From the Coal Mines to the Pulpit

By

Rev. John De Polo

ISBN: 1-4033-4967-3 (e-book)
ISBN 1-4033-4968-1 (Paperback)

This book is printed on acid free paper.

1st Books - rev. 08/15/02

Acknowledgements:

Reverend Dominick DePolo - Encouragement in my Christian walk.

Evelyn Secreto - My sister that led me to the Lord with prayers and determination thru my daughter.

Anna Conch - My sister of support, strength, prayer and love.

Teresa Urtso - Deceased youngest sister for her prayers, support and love.

Mary Karnis - Precious deceased sister and mother that raised her five children alone after being widowed at a young age. A loving sister and mother.

Rose Koontz - My sister that has always lived in Baltimore, that I love and cherish.

Dedications:

To my parents, Francesco and Francesca De Poala - For their patience, love and prayers.

To my wife Doris - For her love and support.

To my daughter Brenda - For the inspiration and completion of this book, and leading me to church.

To my son Frank - For following my foot steps in the ministry.

Table of Contents

To God be the Glory

for all of these Miracles!

From the Coal Mines to the Pulpit

I was born into an Italian family. I have five sisters, a father and mother and my recollection about what was going on happened in 1932. My oldest sister, Evelyn, went to a church, and we were devout Catholics. She went to a meeting and was converted. I remember Evelyn coming to our house saying she received Christ as the Lord and Savior. My father went into spasms. I remember father going to the mines and coming home in the evening and putting on his black shirt. One day someone questioned him about the black shirt and he said, well, as far as he was concerned, his oldest daughter, Evelyn, was dead. She was no longer his daughter. He disowned her because she became Judas and left the Catholic church. And shortly after my sister Evelyn was converted, my mother was converted. She received Jesus Christ as her Lord and Savior, and things really got rosy around the house. Father would take a fit on my mother. He would take a fit on the rest of us because of what my mother and sister were doing. Though it was drastically worrying him, he thought they were out of their heads and just would not accept it. I remember this was in 1932.

It was 1933, father was very strict with me. I have five sisters and my mother had spoiled me rotten. Father warned me about going on the ice to skate. It seemed that the moment his back was turned, I went to the ice and we were ice skating. It was in the month of February. We were skating on this body of water and what we didn't realize was that there was a mine fire, and that is something I will never forget for as long as I live. I was the leader of the group at 13 years of age, and as we were skating on the ice, I fell through this soft spot. I heard my friends scream and yell. I heard them yelling as I went down, down, down into the water. It was something unbelievable. I went down and then came up and banged my head against the ice. The ice wouldn't budge. It was 6-8 inches thick. I then went down again and it seemed as if my body was floating very lifelessly. All of a sudden, I felt strength come into my body. I started swimming upward again and it seemed that there was a compulsion under me, something that was pushing me to the surface, and lo and behold, I came up. I found the same hole I had fallen through. Everybody screamed and yelled. They threw me a rope and then pulled me out of the water. They built a fire and tried to get my clothes dry, because it was in the month of February and it seemed like icicles just formed on my clothes. I realized that the wisest thing to do was to go home. So I did. When I arrived home, I guess father must have been looking down and saw what happened, mother was over at her sisters house and father had my water ready in our bedroom in a #3 wash tub. The water was hot. He helped me get my shoes and clothes off and I got into the tub. It felt so good. It felt like heaven itself, until I got out of the water. After a while when I started drying off, father came into the room with that huge mining belt and, brother, he made huge welts on my behind. I wasn't able to sit for days after that. But I thanked God through it all. I didn't realize it at that moment, but, through it all, God had his hand upon my life. I should have drowned right then and there.

Things went on as usual. Father declared war on mother and my sister Evelyn, because of their conversion. At the age of 17, I started gambling, and drinking. All the vices you could think of. It seemed I loved playing poker. It was in my blood. It seemed I could think of nothing, nothing, nothing else but playing poker. This went on and on and on. At the age of 18, I remember mother saying to me "Don't you think you ought to give your heart to Jesus and give up all these wild things you're doing?" I said, "No, I'm only 18 years of age and I'm too young to start going to church. One of these days I will, but not now."

I remember that I started working in the mines running a locomotive at about this time. One day, while working in the mines, the Snapper came out and he was ill. He said to me, "We're only working 2 days a week and I hate to go home. I have a wife and 3 children. Why not let me run the locomotive, I think I can make it." So, I did that. I let him run the locomotive. After the second trip we made into the mine, it seemed the cars wrecked. I signaled him with my light to pull the cars back toward him. Instead of pulling them back toward him, he pushed them against me and caught me between the cars and crushed my hip. That injury I've carried all my life. As a matter of fact, I cried day and night. I remember for thirty days and thirty nights there was no relief from the pain. There was nothing the doctors could do because they tried everything. They gave me medication but it just didn't kill the pain. One day my mother said to me, "John, I knew that God was going to use you one day. I know that God has his hands upon you and I'm going to start reading my Bible to you. What would you like me to read?" I thought, well with my name being John, "Start with the Gospel of St. John." My pain was so unbearable I could put a pillow between my knees and still feel the pain going from one knee to the other. Every time Mom would pick up the Bible and read to me, that pain would leave. It would actually leave. There would be no more aches, no more pains. I could move my leg around, up and down and it seemed so beautiful. But then mother would say, "Your father is coming home from the mines. I can see him coming up the walkway", and she would have to put her Bible away. Then the pain would return. Then I would say to father, "Aren't you going hunting? Isn't there something you are going to do?" He would say, "No, I'm going to stay home tonight." Then the pain would be there until the next day when father would leave for the mines. Mom would have me up bright and early because I had very little sleep. She would read the Bible again and again. The pain would leave. This went on for quite a while. Then one day I said to my mother, "Mom, I'm going to promise you, I'm going to make a vow to the Lord. If God will permit me to walk, I will turn my heart over to the Lord. I will give him first place in my life and my heart. Mom, I'll go to church with you and do anything you say." She said, "Fine." One week later, lo and behold, I was no longer lying on the bed screaming with pain, the pain having subsided, I was walking.

5

Limping, but walking. Hobbling along and everybody marveled. Before long, it's unbelievable, I went back to work. Then mother said to me, she said, "John, remember the vow you made to the Lord?" I said, "Mom, I know God is good and I'm thankful but I'm too young to go to church. Besides I'll take you any time you want to go." She said, "That was not the agreement. The agreement was you were going to turn you heart over to Jesus and you were going to church with me." I said, "Yes, but I just can't, I can't do that."

My life got worse and worse for a young man 18 1/2 years of age. At the age of 19, I started dating a beautiful young lady by the name of Doris Lindsey from Lumberport, West Virginia. A few months later, in February of 1939, we were married. I remember mother saying to me, "Now is the time to start out your life in the right manner. Now is the time to start going to church. Now is the time to give your heart to Jesus." I said, "Mother, I know you love Doris, she is my wife. You love her very much, but I don't want to go to church. I'm too young." My father thought this was the answer; marrying this lovely lady, and bringing her home. They accepted her as their daughter and this was the answer to all my problems. In 1940, our son was born. We named him after my father, Frank. I remember that day, a day that I'll never forget, how I looked to the Lord and I thanked him for this son; but, I was inebriated. My father and the others, they shunned me because they realized the state I was in as my wife was giving birth to our first child. I came home very inebriated. My father said to me, "Now that you have a son, I pray you'll start going to church with your wife and bring your son up in the right way, in the right manner." I still held on to my vices. I didn't pass the physical for the Army because of the terrible condition with my hip. Although I walked my hip was very, very bad. The doctor said to my wife, "One of these days John will have TB of the bone. I thank God up to this day I haven't.

In 1944, my wife was expecting again. I made a vow that if the child she was carrying was a girl, I would change my ways of living. That same year, 1944, in June, a tornado struck Shinnston, West Virginia. I was working in the mines. After my shift was over, I went home and changed where we lived in Meadowbrook, West Virginia. The barber gave me a haircut and he said to me, "John, I understand you're a pretty good gambler." I thought, "Well I can hold my own with just about anyone." I said, "Well, I think I am." He asked, "Well, are you going to the game in Elam?" I said, "Yes, after you cut my hair, I'm going to go to that game." He said, "Well, I'll tell you what, I'm going to beat you. I'm going to close my shop and I'm going to that game and I'll prove to you that I'm a better poker player than you are." After I left the barbershop, I started toward Elam, which is in Shinnston. After I arrived at the point where I was to cross the railroad tracks to go over into Elam the train was coming with many, many cars. I waited and waited and waited and, after a while, I became very impetuous and said, "I'm not going to wait." So I left for home. I got just about where the Shinnston cemetery is located and changed my mind again. I thought, "Well, I promised the barber I was going to that poker game and I'm going." I turned my car around and headed back to Shinnston. Just as I arrived down where the tracks were, I searched for Elam, my 1935 Plymouth would not go to the left. The wheel would not turn to the left. I drove near the Methodist church, got under the car to see if the tie rods were loose, and there was nothing wrong with the tie rods. I turned the car around. This time turning it to the left and it went to the left. I got down to where the road goes across the railroad tracks in Elam when another train came with many, many cars. This time I said, "Well, I know what I'm going to do. I'm going to forget about the poker game and I'll

8

apologize to the fellow the next time I see him." I went on home. I arrived at Johnny Bart's grocery store. I was there about 5 minutes and I heard the hogs squealing and making terrible noise. Someone said, "I wonder what's going on with those animals?" About 5 minutes later someone came running and said, "A tornado hit Shinnston. Many, many people were killed." Five people jumped into my automobile and we went down to Shinnston. We were there in about 10 minutes. A policeman said we couldn't get through unless we had relatives, so I lied to him and said, "Yes I do. All of my people live in Shinnston." It was a barefaced lie. The policeman parked me next to a streetcar on the left hand side as you enter Shinnston and I looked and, lo and behold, there was a lady's head. I never did see the body. It made me sick to my stomach. I walked into Shinnston and when I got down to the point looking out of Elam, a row of about 25 houses down through there, there wasn't one house standing. Someone said to me, "I thought you were in that tornado?" I said, "No." The barber, Mr. Shreeves was there. I said, well, I promised him I was going to go and told him of my circumstances of why I didn't go and he said, "You're very fortunate. There were 16 people killed in that home. You would have been number 17." I just

9

thanked God again for sparing my life a second time. This was in June.

In September 1944, our daughter was born. A little baby girl. We named her, or I did, Brenda. What I had promised I was going to do, I did. I promised I would stop my gambling, stop my drinking and we started going to church. Reverend Corsini baptized my wife and I on June 3, 1949, my birthday. After 2 1/2 years of going to church, things got bad again. Things got really bad. It seemed now that Doris and I were on the verge of divorce and we had 2 children. My father was very concerned about me. My older sister, Evelyn, was really concerned. My sister, Evelyn, married Pat Secreto. My next oldest sister, Ann, married John Conch. My sister Rose was still with us at the time when things were really bad. The Reverend Corsini left the Clarksburg Church and moved to Pittsburgh and, for all intense purposes, I thought, "Well, maybe I should continue to go to church." Then a gentleman by the name of Reverend Dominick DePolo became pastor of the Clarksburg Church. Before that, I believe in 1949, my wife had surgery and I thought we were going to lose her. She was having convulsions and it seemed the doctors gave us no hope and a Baptist Minister came on the scene. He came to visit Dot, as I call her in the hospital and, shortly after that, she got better. What I didn't know, Dot had committed herself to the Lord. After that Reverend Corsini came on the scene and, as I said, we had attended the church for about 2 1/2 years. Then it seemed that overnight, Satan really got a hold of me again and we stopped going to church. This man, Reverend DePolo, tried dealing with us. I was no longer working at Hutchison Coal Company and went to work at Dawson Coal Company. While working there, the Devil would tip me off every time Reverend DePolo was going to come to our house. I would come home from work and drive up to where my sister Mary lived. Mary married a gentleman by the name of Alex Karnis. She lived about a 1/2 mile from where we lived. From their house I could look down and see my garage and see if there was anyone in the driveway. I would see Reverend DePolo's car pull up. I would watch him pull up. After about an hour and a half he would pull away. He did this many, many times. Things got worse and worse and my father pleaded with Reverend DePolo to see what he could do with me. Finally in 1953, my daughter Brenda said to me on a Saturday night, "Are you going to church tomorrow?" I said "No I'm not going to church. I'll drive you and grandma and Aunt Evelyn." She said, "No.

If you don't go to church, then I'm not going." That was one of the worst Saturday nights and Sundays I believe I ever had. The following Saturday I said to Brenda, "Are you going to church?" She said, "No daddy. If you don't go to church, I don't want to go." She said, "That's final. I've made up my mind. Unless you go to church, I'm not going." Brenda had long braids. I said to my wife, "Well, you'd better fix her hair because tomorrow we're all going to church." I later found out that my eldest sister Evelyn, had coached Brenda to cry and refuse to go to church without me. I thank God for my sisters loving care and prayers for me.

So, in 1953, we all started going to church. Shortly after we started again, our church had a revival. Back then if it was called a revival, it was a revival. A young man, fresh out of Bible School, by the name of Phillip Bongiorno, came to our Clarksburg Assembly and held a 2 week revival. During the 2 weeks, 18 of the DePolo family got saved. I remember one night, Doris had received a baptism the night before, I kept telling my brother-in-law Pat Secreto that I was going to receive the baptism of the Holy Spirit. He said, "No you can't because you've been too bad. God's not going to baptize you." I remember we went to church together and Pat was with us. When we got to the church, Brother Phillip Bongiorno said to me, "Brother Johnny, tonight is your night. God is going to fill you with the baptism of the Holy Spirit." I thought, "Well, that's what I've been praying for." This was a Saturday night and on Sunday night the meetings would close. So, that night, I remember going to the altar, praying to God, crying, crying, crying and my brother-in-law right beside me praying "Oh Lord, fill me with your spirit. Don't make me suffer, don't made me suffer." That's all he could say and to me it was quite a distraction. Then Brother Phillip came over and laid his hand on me and said, "Brother Johnny, God is going to fill you with his spirit and God is going to move upon you." Shortly after that, the power of the Holy Spirit fell upon me. I felt my tongue getting so thick and I could hardly speak. In a few minutes, I found myself speaking in a language I had never heard. Then I remember the blessings God has sent upon me. Just shortly after that, I heard someone hit the floor and I knew who it was because my brother-in-law didn't believe in that. He didn't believe, he wanted to do everything decently in order and God surely wouldn't do it that way but, you know, God had to teach him a lesson. Pat fell to the floor and I heard him speak in other tongues. In March of 1953, the scales were removed from my eyes. I thanked God first, my daughter second. She refused to go to church without me.

My daughter would go to work with me when I sold sweepers, her job was to pour dirt from a large bag so that my Electrolux would clean it up as a demonstration. One day Brenda got frightened, she said "Daddy what will happen to you if the sweeper doesn't work and the dirt is left on the ladies carpet?" I explained to her about having faith in the Lord, she understood and was happy that I would be ok!

March 12, 1953, 18 of our family were saved. Doris and I were baptized with the Holy Spirit. Shortly after that, a man by the name of Albert Seals, that I used to gamble with, everybody knew him as Al Seals, everyone was afraid of him because he was big and I thought he was loony because I saw him use his razor a few times on people, this black man, Al Seals, one day walked up to me and said, "You know, I heard you're going to church? I heard you got saved?" I said, "Yes." He then said, "I'm thrilled to death. I'm thrilled to hear you got saved because now I can rest in peace." I said, "What are you talking about?" He pulled out his razor and hit the switchblade. The thing looked a foot long but was 8 inches long. He said, "I've watched every move that you've made and knew every habit you had. When we played poker together you didn't play straight, you were cheating. I never saw you cheat but figured you did. I'm glad you got saved because I was going to cut your throat from ear to ear." I thank God I got saved.

In the later part of 1954, I got laid off from work. I was never laid off before. My wife had to go to work. She got a job at the Working Mans Store, first at W.T.. Grants Store then at the Working Mans Store, so we could survive. I remember shortly after that one day, the Electrolux man, one of the bosses, came by and said to me, "You know, I think you have the ability to become a good salesman." I said to him, "How do you know?" He said, "Because you have the ability, you have the looks and you have everything that goes with it." A lady, one of our friends, came to visit us, one of the Job's converters. You know I just bought a new automobile in 1952. I said, "How are you?" She said, "Well, I have a word for you. I hope you'll take it kindly. I believe you may lose your home, may lose your automobile and God may be just testing you." I said, "Why would god test me? Why would He cost me my home, my automobile and all? I don't believe that." Then I said to her, "You know, I serve a God of love, not a God of misery." So, I started selling sweepers. The first week I went to school, the second they sang a song. I forget the name of the song but, man, it would really make the adrenaline flow through your body. I remember the third week. I went out and sold 3 sweepers. Then the next week and next week and the next week I sold. Finally I became on e of the best salesman that they had. The man said to me, "Well John, you know, I believe you're going to be number one salesman." I said to him, he was a Jewish man, "I'm sorry, I'm going to have to give you 2 weeks notice." He said to me, "I'll talk to your wife." I said, "I'm not talking about my wife, I'm talking about the boss., the man upstairs said to me that my home is paid off and my automobile is paid off and now that I'm on my feet again I need to study the word of God because he wants me to Minister." He thought I was one of the most foolish men he had ever met. Then it seems one day shortly after that, I started studying for the Ministry, a young man by the name of Johnny Mancini who helped me much in my studies and Reverend DePolo was a wonderful Bible teacher and I went to every service that our church held and I thanked God for this man because I learned so very much from him. Then one day it was on a Saturday, I'll never forget it, I went squirrel hunting with my father, and my brother-in-law's Pat Secreto and John Conch. When we got to Jane Lew, West

Virginia which was about 35 miles from where we lived. We went into the woods about 6:00 in the morning when we arrived. We left home at 4:30. We parked the car at some peoples home and we went up on the hill. It seemed for once in my life I couldn't hit anything I shot at. I just couldn't hit any squirrels at all. About 10:00 in the morning I left the woods and sat in my automobile, and while sitting in my automobile I was trying to pick up the Italian language. I had an Italian and English Bible. On the left page was the English and on the right was the Italian. When I was doing this, a lady came out of the home and she said, "sir, are you a minister?" and I said, "no, I'm not". She said, "my mother-in-law is very ill and she needs a minister." After she went back in the house I found out later her name was Annabelle Lipps. It seemed that I was going to have a heart attack, my heart was beating up in my throat and misery through my chest and I thought "Lord, if that's you speaking to me for me to go into that house, then have that woman come out again." No sooner said than done. The woman comes out and she is pretending to put water around her rose bushes and I said to her, I said, "ma'am, I'd like to go in and talk to your mother-in-law." She said, "I thought you weren't a minister?" I said, "I'm not but I would like to talk to her." So, she

17

invited me in and opened the door for me and I went in. When I got in, I saw a lady sitting in a rocking chair, tied to the rocking chair. I said to her, "how are you", she said, "I'm not feeling to good. I've had surgery and my incision doesn't want to heal and the doctor doesn't give me any hope." I said to her, "do you know Jesus as your savior?" She said, "No, but I would like to know him. I've been taking lessons from a man in California over the radio. I listened to his program. This man has been trying to teach me how to get saved and I've been sending him $10.00 a week for 4 years and thus far, I don't know anymore than I did when I first started listening to him." Then she said, "Will you help me?" I said, "yes." I opened my Bible to the book of Romans, chapter 10 and I read to her from St. John and Nicademous encounter with Christ, and then I said to her, "All you have to do is except the word of God and I'm going to pray for you and ask Jesus to come into your heart and in your life. In 2 minutes it was all over and she said, "Yes, yes, yes, I want to receive God as my savior." And she did. Then with my hunting togs and all I said to her, "The same God that saved you is going to heal you." Once again I knelt and got on my knees and put her hands in mine and I prayed that the Lord would heal her body. Then I excused myself and I went

18

outside. A few minutes later the daughter-in-law Annabelle came running out and she said, "Mr., I don't know who you are but I want you to come back in." So I went into the house. The lady that was sitting in the rocking chair tied down, was no longer tied down. She changed clothes. What I didn't know was that she had a cancer operation on the mid section of her stomach and it wouldn't heal. After I went outside the daughter-in-law came running through the house and she said "Ma, Ma, did you feel that, I could feel it in the backroom." That was the end of the conversation and I left the room. Then when she came back and said to me, "I want you to come back." I went in and I saw this lady standing on her feet. She said to me, "Mr., you have the old fashioned gospel. Jesus Christ is still alive isn't he, because he saved me and healed my body. I'll tell you something else, if you'd like, you can come up here tonight and I can have 20 people attend the service and I'll tell them about what happened to me and I'm sure that many of them will be saved." I said, "Fine, I'll do just that." I remember my father, my two brother-in-laws and myself driving all the way back to Meadowbrook and then I said, "I think I'm coming back up here tonight." My father said to me, "Why are you coming back up here. You can't shoot and hit squirrels

19

in the daytime, are you going to do it at night?" I said, "No, I'm coming up here because tonight we're going to have a service up here." So, after we arrived home, I told my wife what happened. I told her that we were going to go back and we were going to have a service there that night. So my wife Doris, my niece Jean, Ernest Knight, and myself, went to Berlin, West Virginia. They had quite a number of folk there. There was a lady that attended that meeting, Annabelle Lipps' mother, she said, "I think you've done about all your going to do here, but if you'll come to my home, I live at the other end of this road which is about 10 miles from here. To get to my place, you will have to go through Buchannan, and just as you top Gum Mountain you'll turn right at Volga and go down over the hill. It is the white house. I'll have my lights on. I guarantee you 40 people will be at that service." So the following Saturday we went to Volga, West Virginia. Sure enough, the lady's name was Mrs. Spores. She had a husband and a daughter, Virgie Spores, and she had three sons. They attended the meeting and many, many other people attended. So, we started our mission work there. The third Saturday we were there, we had a family by the name of Cutright. Ralph Cutright and his wife Goldie. They came to the meeting and he said to me, "You know, I have a sister that has cancer. I heard that Lipp's mother was healed and I'm going to tell my sister, her name is Jennabe D. Landers. I'm going to tell her to come down and I want you to pray to her." That following Saturday, sure enough, we went to the meeting and there were 2 rooms filled with people. I'll never forget it, as we entered the room I could smell the terrible odor of cancer. The lady came up to me, her eyes red because she was crying. She said the doctors have given me 2 weeks to live. But, I heard how you pray for people and how God heals them. I've come here tonight and I have 5 of my children with me and I know when you pray that God is going to heal me." I'm now thinking to myself, "Well, if God is going to heal you, then why doesn't he tell me?" Then I thought, "Who am I?, I'm a nobody." Then we went into the service and shortly after the service was over, my wife and another lady, Louie Frats wife, and then Louis Frat and others prayed for this lady. And it seemed everybody was crying. Then I said to her, "If you'll come up now, we're going to pray for you." When she came up I had to put a handkerchief over my mouth and my nose so I wouldn't smell that Terrible stench. Just as I anointed her with oil, I closed my eyes and I couldn't smell a thing. I followed with my prayer. I prayed that the Lord would heal her. Just

21

about the end of the prayer she started screaming and yelling and crying and jumping. She had a patch over the outward hole in her chest. She pulled the patch off and lo and behold, her flesh was like a child's flesh, two tone. Jennabe was in her late 40's and here she had a baby like flesh that came over the hole she had. She was healed instantly of cancer. Now that really started something, because the next Saturday we went up, we had so many people that attended that we couldn't get them all in the house. It reminded me when Jesus was on the Sea of Gallilee and in the boat and the people gathered on the seashore to hear what he had to say. So, we were standing on the porch of that long home and the people that gathered around, they were listening to the word of God. There was a young man that came, and to this day I don't know his name, but I'm sure that God does. This young man, what we didn't realize that years ago we called it St. Vidas dance, but it's Parkinsons Disease, and this young man was told by the doctor that this was what he had. He was 24-25 years of age. He had just gotten married 2 weeks before that. I noticed that he was at our service 2 or 3 times before that. He said to me, "I believe that when you people pray for me that something is going to take place." We prayed for him. After we prayed, someone brought it to my

22

attention that his hands was no longer shaking and the quivering had stopped and God had healed him instantly. After that, we never saw him again. We continued with our meetings up there. God performed many miracles. I'm only going to get into the highlights of the mission. Mrs. Lipp's, the daughter-in-law, that invited me to the first meeting, came down to her, "Annabelle, I hate to say this but your TB is going to spread to your children and your husband. I have no alternative, so I'm going to have to send you away to the Hopemont Sanitarium. I'm going to send you there on a Monday. You come to my office and the bus will be there. You'll get on the bus and go to Hopemont." So, she came to our meeting and she cried and cried and we prayed for her. For me to say that I knew that God had healed her, I wouldn't be telling the truth. I felt absolutely nothing. We prayed for her. We anointed her with oil and we believed that Jesus Christ was the same Yesterday, today, and forever. Then we went on our way and they went on their way. The next time we met, the story was told. On the Monday, preceding that Saturday, Rally Lipps, who was a coal miner, went to the doctors office with his wife and said, "Before my wife boards this bus to go to the Sanitarium, my wife was anointed with oil by the same man that prayed for my mother and prayed for

23

Ms. Landers and healed them both from cancer. He prayed for my wife that you would find absolutely nothing wrong with her lungs. And the doctor said to him, "Rally, your wife's lungs are riddled like she has been shot with a shotgun. I don't believe that there is any change in her, but if you'll pay for the bill then I will x-ray her." So the doctor took the first x-ray, he took the second, and took the third. Then he looked at the x-ray when it was still wet. He was smoking a cigarette. Rally Lipps said the cigarette fell out of his mouth. He came in sat down and talked for a minute and then went back to look at the x-ray. He said, "You know, I didn't believe this, I still don't know what to say, but I do know that your wife doesn't have TB. You can take her home and take care of those kids." That was the beginning of the beginning in Volga, West Virginia.

When the Lord blesses, you can look forward everytime, the devil sets up his Tent meeting. The following Saturday, after Mrs. Lipps was healed, Doris didn't go with us this time because she wasn't feeling too well, so Jean, my niece, Jean Conch, Evelyn Secreto, Mrs. Barlow, Theresa Perry, and John Locante and I want. Brother John Locante said to me, "Brother DePolo, we're going to kick Satan in his pants. God is really going to bless in this service." I thought so too because I had spent 6 hours in prayer in our Clarksburg church crying out to the Lord to save people, to heal sick bodies, and while I was praying, God gave me a message and it's in second Peter 2-22. What is happening to them according to the true proverb, the dog is turned to his own vomit again the sow that washed wallowed in the mire. God gave me that message, but when we arrived up there, instead of having 60-80 people, there were only about 20-24 people. I thought, "who am I going to preach this sermon to?" So, I said well, I thought to my self, we're going to pray and sing a few choruses and then we're going to dismiss with prayer and we're going home because it's 0 degree weather outside. Not too many people came out and why prolong things because the people here are surely saved and they've been coming here for a few months. Now that was my way of thinking. No I knelt down and God spoke to me again with that small voice. He said, "You've received the word today when you were praying. You preached that word." I'm a very obstinate person when it comes to obeying at times. I stood to my feet and I thought well, I know what we're going to do. We're going to sing a few choruses. We're going to ask for Testimony or two then we're going to close with prayer and then we'll be on our way home. The spirit of God spoke to me again. This time I had that same sensation I had when I went in to pray for grandma Lipps. My heart started beating furiously and I thought well Lord, I know your trying to get through to me this hard headed Calabreze, I know what I'll do. I'll preach what you gave me today. The sermon is about 15 minutes long. About a Christian that was known of the Lord and gone back into the world then Satan takes over and that person is pitiful, they wallow again in the mire like the dog that returns to his vomit and so forth and so on. I thought after it was all said and done, why did I preach such a foolish sermon to anyone but Christians. Then I said to my niece, "Will you go over and pray with this young man." He was sitting on my far right. I was going to pray with somebody on my far left. All of a sudden, the spirit of God said, "You pray with him." So, I went over and spoke with him. His name is Harold K. Hall. I said, "Harold, Jesus loves you. I'm sure you love the Lord." I laid my hands on his shoulder and I felt a sensation. I felt this young man had power in his life. But, little did I realize who this power was coming from. I said to him, "Harold, I realized that there is something going on here that I can't figure out. Harold, you need deliverance. Call on the name of the Lord." And as sure as my name is John, my wife had bought me a new hat that day when I went in to pick her up at the Working Mans store and I wore the hat to the meeting and the hat was overlooking the young man to the far right. I could see my hat. I said to him, "Harold, call on the name of the Lord and he will deliver you." He said, "Jesus help me." He went through the air, and I'm not exaggerating, at least 15 feet. Lo and behold he hits the stand that my hat was on 15 feet away and it fell down by his leg and I reached down to pick up my hat. He kicked me in the leg. My, my, I wanted to retaliate and kick back, but I thought I can't do that because I'm a Christian. So, after it was all said and done, we started to pray. I realized that there was something strange about this young man, he's coming at us with his feetlike a kicking mule. I said, that the thing to do was to hold onto him. So, 5 of the young men and Mr. Spores was holding this young man down. He weighed about 140 pounds. The five of them weighed about 750-800 pounds. It's unbelievable, he was carrying them around like toys. I realized that this was the supernatural power of the Devil. Brother Locante, the one that said we were going to kick the Devil tonight, laid his hand on him and he kicked him in the stomach. Oh, my did he hurt him. I said to him, I said, "brother, you go over and kneel and pray." Someone said, "brother Johnny, should we turn him loose and pray?" I said, "If we turn him loose, he'll kill all of us, the best thing to do is pray." After about an hour of praying and calling on the name of the Lord and people crying, the gentleman that owned the home had 3 sons and they ran wild. They ran out of the house into the night because they realized that this young man was demon possessed. After it was all said and done, and after praying and praying, I spoke to the Lord. I said, "Lord, unless you deliver him, our work up here is finished. People will hear about this and they won't come to anymore services and we'll be done." About 5 seconds after that, the Lord put it on my heart to lay my Bible on him. I laid my Bible on him and I could hear the Demon's screaming "No, no." They screamed and screamed. I said to him, "Harold, call on the name of the Lord." He was like a mute, he just couldn't speak or even open his mouth. Then I was so tired and fatigued I sat down in the chair by the fireplace. I looked up and lo and behold this young man carried those 6 men to the fireplace. The Devil was going to put his head in the fire. Then I put my foot against his head and I turned it away. Then once again, I put my Bible on him and I said, "Harold, call on the name of the Lord." For seven straight times, he called on the name of the Lord and for seven straight times, his head and face hit the floor. After the seventh time, I said let him alone. Now he was lifeless on the floor. Then I said to the gentlemen, "pick him up and lay him on the couch." God had marvelously delivered him. He did not need to go to the hospital or Psychiatric doctor. Jesus Christ had delivered him safely and completely from those demons. Two days later, Harold Hall wrote me a letter. It said, "Brother DePolo, the reason I was kicking like I was, was because Satan had me in Hell and I was kicking to get out. I'm sorry that I stomped on your hat. I'm sorry that I kicked Brother Locante and I'm sorry that I kicked Sister Barlow because I love you people and I know people love me. I'm sorry that Satan was the great deceiver and there was a time that I was really saved and on fire for the Lord, but then I permitted Satan to come in. When he came in, he brought these 7 Demons that I've been living with for 2 years. But, I thank God, that he has delivered me and set me free. Shortly after this, we moved our work to Volga, West Virginia or Phillipi, West Virginia. A little church on the wrong side of the tracks and incidentally Phillipi, West Virginia, during the Civil War, was the town where the first shot was fired. That's where we set up our church. Before we went to Phillipi and Volga, West Virginia, after 6 months of going to this building, we saw a young lady saved and filled with the spirit of God one night while we were praying. I saw her kiss the floor and shortly after that, I heard her speaking in other tongues. I said to her, her name was Mabel Campbell, "Mabel, explain something to me, why did you kiss the floor?" She said, "I did not kiss the floor, I kissed Jesus's feet. He was standing by the water right there by that little tree." And, she opened her eyes up and didn't realize that he had taken her into the spirit when he filled her with the spirit. Mabel went home because we were praying for the others to receive the Baptism of the Holy Spirit. Mabel had to pass by our neighbors home to get home and the neighbor said to her, "Mabel, I don't know what t is but there is something surely different about you. Your face has a glow on it." Shortly after that in our Sunday School, we had an attendance of 97. Frank, my son was in Bible College. I remember when Frank went away to Bible School, it was 1958. My father was very, very ill and Frank was reluctant. He wanted to go and he didn't want to go. Shortly after that our work really grew. Now, I was laid off at the mines again and I started working on the State road, painting tall bridges. In my work on the road, I witnessed everyone I met. I remember we went to a little town by the name of Rollsburg, West Virginia. We painted the tall bridge there. We stayed at the hotel and Ms. Howard owned the hotel. What they didn't put me through. I guess I cried out to the Lord, I couldn't see anything but Mountains in the daytime or night. I cried out to the Lord, I didn't want to be with these ungodly people. But the Lord was teaching me. These men would gather night after night after hours were over, and I would take my bible and I would hold onto it with all my heart. These men would go downstairs into the room and play poker. One night they invited me to go down and play with them. I went down and I took my Bible with me and I started reading my Bible out loud and before it was over, I broke up the poker game. The same thing over and over again. And then a young man by the name of James Mutis, he was the welder of our crew, he's the one that welded the bridges before we painted, he said to me and to the others, "you know, I'm going to pull a good one on John. I'm gong to get a bottle of liquor and I'm gong to tell him to baptize me and every once in awhile I'm gonna put my head under the covers and take a drink of the whiskey and I'm going to make a fool out of him. They said to me, "James is ill and he wants you to go to his room." I said, "what's wrong with him?" They said, "he's ill and he's in bed." So I went up and said, "what's the problem?" He said, "I don't feel good. I feel like I'm

31

going to die. I wish you would Baptize me in water. We'll put water in the bathtub and you can Baptize me." I said, "well, before I Baptize you, you have to have a change of heart." Then he put his head under the cover and I could hear the gurgling. Finally after the third time around I said, "Jimmy, my Bible tells me God is not mocked. Whatever a man sows, he also reaps." And, he became so deathly ill that they drove him home the next day. He went to the hospital. Two weeks later he returned to work with us and he said to everybody, "Don't you ever make fun of John and don't you ever say anything about his God or the Gospel he preaches, because I thought I was going to die. I will never say anything about this man or about his God. And, I don't want you to say anything about his God." It seemed that Jim had learned his lesson. I was still working on the State road and I remember one day that a man who was related to my mother suffered a severe stroke. He couldn't walk and was admitted to St. Mary's hospital in Clarksburg, West Virginia. I went to visit him, his name was Sam Marra. God was once again going to perform a miracle. My father would say to me, "Why do you bother with Sam Marra. Don't you know that he doesn't want to be bothered." I said, "well, he smiles at me and he shakes my hand." After awhile they discharged Sam Marra from the hospital because they sent him home to die. I would go to his home after work about every evening after church and it seemed that Sam was on the verge of going. But he was going to go without Christ. I thought, well I'm going to do everything in my power to make sure that this man makes it into heaven. So I said to him, "Sam, I'm going to pray that God will save you." He looked at me and he smiled. "Then I'm going to pray that God will heal you." I laid my hands on him and he couldn't say anything because he couldn't speak. I prayed and the first thing I know, I hear Sam Marra's up walking. Shortly after that he regained his speech. He went around telling everybody that Jesus Christ moved upon him, quickened him, but, John DePolo healed him. I said to him, "Sam, it's very embarrassing telling people I healed you. I didn't heal you. Jesus Christ healed." John Bart, the man that owned the grocery store said to him the same thing, "No, no, he didn't heal you. Jesus Christ healed you Sam." Nevertheless, Sam was pig headed. He told the people John DePolo healed him and now he was thinking about going to John DePolo's church. He had a son by the name of Frank, whom I grew up with. After I received Christ and the Lord as my savior he had nothing to do with me. Then one day I said to Sam, "Sam, don't you think it's about time you came out openly for Christ and tell people that Christ saved you and Christ healed you and that you are going to start going to church somewhere where you can get your soul fed. You're welcome to come with us because I have a station wagon and I have plenty of room." He said, "I would love to come to your church John, but my son Frank already told me that he would spit in my face. I just can't have my family do that to me. If I was younger, yes, I would come. Now, I'm old and I just can't do that now. So, you'll have to forgive me." It seemed that Sam just wouldn't go. Later on, they moved to Ohio and I lost touch with Sam Marra. Then I heard a few years later after we moved to Washington, Pennsylvania that Sam came to Washington on Memorial day to place flowers on his wife's grave and just as he bent over to put the wreath on his wife's grave he dropped dead. That was the end of that. Then his son Frank, who I went to school with and buddied together with and when he was in the service, my we did everything in our power for him, I heard he had cancer. I went up to visit him before he passed away. I was able to reach him with the Gospel of Jesus Christ, and his brother John was there present to see all of this. So, God really moved in marvelous and a miraculous way.

And then it seemed one Saturday night that we just couldn't get to go to the mission. I always had fear that my father was going to leave this life without Christ. I prayed and I cried out to the Lord. Seemingly nothing happened, but this Saturday we just didn't go to the mission and I invited Reverend DePolo to come down to visit with Daisy Barlow. She sang and we held a prayer service in our home. Father came over, and lo and behold I saw my father get on his knees and I saw tears streaming down his cheeks. Reverend DePolo went over to him and I saw my father receive Jesus Christ as his Lord and Savior. Praise the name of the Lord! Doesn't the Bible say that God will save us and our household. We need to hold on to that and we need to believe that. We need to believe that Jesus Christ is the same yesterday, today, and forever because he is. It seemed that after my father got saved, he got worse and worse. The more I prayed it seemed the sicker he became. Our work in Volga I felt it was coming to a close and I didn't know what to expect next. One day I received a card from Reverend Corsini, who is the general secretary of the Christian Churches of the North America, asking me if I would come to Cannonsburg, Pennsylvania and fill in for the church of Canonsburg until they got a Pastor. So the first Sunday I went alone.

Our son Frank was there from Bible college and he was there and I said to my wife and son that on Saturday I would go over there and stay with someone and then on Sunday I would go to church.

Sunday after the service was over, I was on my way home and I said, "God I thank you that you didn't ask me to come to this place and preach the Gospel of Jesus Christ." Meanwhile, back at home, God was revealing to Doris that he was calling me away from Phillipi, West Virginia to Canonsburg, Pennsylvania and there if I would obey God's call on my life, there is where I would Pastor. My wife told our son about what had happened and what had taken place. Our son who is very wise looked at his mother and said please don't tell dad. At least not now.

Then Frank went onto Bible school. Then I came home. I remember after I became a Christian I used to read 80 to 90 chapters a day. I had such a hunger for the word of God. I loved to pray. Many times when I'd drive my wife to work, my wife and my niece Jean, I would go to the church and pray. Then when it was time to pick them up in the evening, I would go to the church and pick them up. Very few people knew this, but there were days I would pray 6, 7, and 8 hours. Even at home. My father and I became close after I became a Christian. My father said to my mother one day. He said, "I'm glad our son has really changed." She said, "Have you noticed?" He said, "sure I've noticed. I've seen him change from daylight to dark, from dark to daylight. I like what I see. I know that God has his hand upon my son and one of these days he'll get the best job he's ever had." As time went on, there was John Masto, and William Holts, another young man, the 3 of us were in the same church and we're wanting God to use us. I would go up into my attic at home and I would pray. Father would look for me and I would hear the door open and close and he couldn't find me. Then I'd come down from the attic and he would say, "Where were you?" I would say, I was upstairs doing something. Then he would look at me and grin because he knew I was praying. Then I'd go to church and pray. Once day when I was in church praying, I could hear someone upstairs. I ran up to look through the keyhole and there was my Brother John Masto. He was up front and he was preaching to the pews. Oh, my, was he preaching a message to the pews. Hell, fire and brimstone. Then another time I remember about John. I came into the church and he was upstairs and I thought well, I'll go down in the boiler room, down where the furnace is. I turned the light on and after awhile I got to praying so much that I could no longer hear John upstairs. After about 3 yours, I stood to my feet and I raised my hand and I said Lord Jesus, take my hand, and I touched that lightbulb. For a moment I thought that someone did take my hand. It was a long time before I'd raise my hand again. Then I remember many, many beautiful things about Brother John Masto and Brother William Holts. But, behind it all, there was a gentleman by the name of Dominick DePolo who really wanted to see God use these 3 young men and he stuck behind us through thick and thin. He did everything in his power to encourage and strengthen us. Little did we realize that Dominick's hand was upon us, and until this day I thank Jesus Christ who is alive for evermore for sending Brother Dominick DePolo our way because if a man has ever suffered from the Gospel of Jesus Christ was this man and I never heard him say a word about throwing up his hands, about giving up, but this man always set his face like a flint and made up his mind where he wanted to go. And that's where he went. I thank God for the Christian Church of N. America an organization who has stood behind it's ministers, an organization who has blessed it's ministers, an organization who has always come to our aid. I remember when they put a write-up in our paper, in our Vista, or the lighthouse at that time, about our work in

Phillipi, West Virginia, how God had blessed. We had a gentleman in Phillipi, West Virginia who was 89 years of age and unsaved. One day I said to him, "Uncle George, don't you want to see your wife?" He said, "Yes, I know my wife has gone to heaven and one day I'm going to see her." I said, "You can't." He said, "Why not?" I said because you don't know Jesus Christ as your Lord and Savior." Right then and there, this man fell to his knees and asked Jesus Christ to come into his heart and into his life at the age of 89. Then in that same home in Volga, West Virginia, we went up on a Saturday evening and I noticed the daughter Vergy wasn't in our service. I said to her mother, "Where is Vergy?" She said, "Vergy has Rheumatic fever. She is upstairs in bed and please don't go up because if you upset her and something happens, I'm going to blame you." I winked at my niece Jean and we both went up. We prayed with her and she said, "I think I'm going to get out of bed." I said, "Don't you do that because your mom will take a fit on me if you do." So we left and she made this promise to me, she said, "You know Brother Johnny, next Saturday when you come up for your meeting, I'm going to sit downstairs where I usually sit and enjoy it." So, the following Saturday we went up and lo and behold, Vergy was sitting in the

39

service. Then we found out that 2 months later she was married. The doctor said that her blood was better than his. God had healed her of Rheumatic fever. The father was very, very ill with Brights disease, a kidney disease that was fatal. He go so bad that we thought that this was it. On a Saturday night, Brother John Masto was with us and I had him speak and after he preached we had a lady from Buckhannan, West Virginia who joined us by the name of Madalyn Woods. Madalyn was singing a song, Oh Tell Me His Name, oh I'm glad I know his name, and his name is Jesus Christ, but as Madalyn was singing this song she would go into tongues and then she would give us this song again. She would repeat this song over and over again. Finally we knelt down and held hands around Mr. Spore and I saw something that night I never seen before or everafter, Mr. Spore was lying on his bed. He had chewing tobacco in his mouth and Brother John Masto looked at him and said, "Brother, do you want God to heal you, spit that tobacco out." Mr. Spores asked for a can and he spit his tobacco out. Then we started to pray. Then Madalyn started to sing again, oh, Tell Me His Name, the power of God fell. As I said I've never seen it before or after, that bed did not move but the mattress started moving up and down and up and down. I would say

Mr. Spores is quite dizzy now, and not only that but he was having the time of his life. Everytime he went up and down the healing powers would touch him. After it was all said and done, everybody believed Mr. Spores was healed. Mr. Spores believed it also. I said to my wife, "Monday, instead of going to work, you and I are going to drive to Volga, West Virginia and we're going to go up and see if Mr. Spores is really healed before we tell about this miracle." That day we drove to Volga, West Virginia. Doris didn't go to work. She went with me to Volga, West Virginia. She went there many, many times after work. I'd pick her up after work and she would go with me. Jean, my niece was always there and ready. My sister Evelyn, oh, she was another one. Then sister Barlow and sister Masto and Sister Perry, they were always there. This particular time, I'm talking about when the healing power hit Mr. Spores and Doris and I went up that Monday. It was Monday afternoon and we were driving down over the hill and I looked up on that hillside of Gum Mountain and I saw a gentleman up there and he had 2 bags of something he was carrying on his shoulder. I thought, it surely couldn't be him because he couldn't be that strong. Even if he was healed Saturday, this is only Monday. As we neared the house, I looked up against the hill again

41

and his wife said, "Do you know who that is there coming down, it's my husband." God has truly healed him, and he had went back to work at the mines. Only the power of God can do these mighty things and I'm glad that I was an instrument that God could use for his honor and for his glory in Volga, in Phillipi, West Virginia, and in that home in Berlin. God is looking for us to do small things. And if we are obedient in the small things, the larger things will come our way and if we're not, they will never come our way. Praise the name of the Lord.

The first miracle I saw was in our home. In Meadowbrook, West Virginia our daughter Brenda was very, very ill with a high fever. The doctor came and wanted to give her a shot and the shot didn't help. Then the Pastor came down and prayed for her. Then Brother Holts, who was working in Shinnston at the time, he stopped by on his way home from work and he prayed for her. Doris and I took turns staying up with Brenda because of her fever. She just couldn't sleep or rest. Then the second night while we were praying, I said to my wife, "Go and lie down for awhile and I'm going to pray with Brenda." After praying with her for about 15 minutes, I prayed and I prayed, "Oh, Lord Jesus, please perform this miracle in my daughters life, you know I love you and you know she loves you Lord and she is the reason I'm serving you Lord. She is the one Lord. She is the one who listened to my sister Evelyn, when my sister Evelyn said, "Tell your daddy you're not going to church unless he does." my sister Evelyn fasted and prayed for her husband to be saved, within the night he was saved, God saved me, the only brother she has. Which means God will do exceedingly and above that in which we ask. As I continued to pray for Brenda, all of a sudden I felt her forehead and it felt cool. The spirit of the Lord had healed her body. This was the first miracle I had ever witnessed with my own eyes. God had healed her and I screamed and yelled and my wife jumped up and came into the room and lo and behold Brenda was sitting up. The fever was broken. God had really undertaken.

Next I want to tell about my calling. I remember driving Doris and Jean to the Working Man's store. On my way back I stopped at my sister Anne's home like I did quite frequently. I walked into her basement where she was washing clothes. I could hear someone call my name, "John", I turned around and looked and she did too. The second time my sister looked at me because she was wiser than I was in the things of God because she was saved longer than I was. She looked at me and she said, "Do you know what that is, that's God calling you into the ministry." It was shortly after that, one night we went to bed and it was in the winter time, we had a 70,000 BTU heating furnace in our living room and it heated the whole house. From our bedroom I could look into the living room and see our lamp and the radio. I had a dream how I was in my vices again. Gambling and drinking and smoking and doing all the other things and it woke me up. I sat up in bed and looked into the living room and I couldn't see the lamp and I knew that there was something wrong. I lay back in bed again and I sat up for the second time and I looked and saw a strange creature. The most beautiful head of hair I had ever seen. Down to his waist. He turned and looked at me. I thought "My God, Satan." I lay back in bed again. I had fear and was trembling. I sat up in bed again and I said, "Satan, I rebuke you in the name of Jesus Christ." I lay down again, and then I sat up again and lo and behold he was gone. I jumped up and I screamed at the top of my voice. My wife sleeping next to me didn't hear a thing and she is a light sleeper. I jumped up and I ran into my daughters room to check if she was alright. I went into my sons room to see if he was alright. They were fine. I realized the next day, we were working in Fairmont, West

Virginia, this was in '54, on the way home someone said to me, "I need you", I turned around and looked and the gentleman looked at me and said, "What are you looking at me for?" I said, "Oh, nothing". I realized that wasn't him. I lay back down again and I'm praying and praying and a strange small voice spoke again and said, "I need you, I want you". Then I realized that it was the Lord Jesus Christ. I had goose bumps up and down my spine, up and down my back, and up and down my legs. It was the Lord calling me into the ministry. That night I believe was the best night that I ever had because I believe I praised the Lord in bed, out of bed,, on my feet, on my back, on my knees. I just couldn't get enough of praising the Lord. Shortly after that, I told a gentleman, a minister friend of ours in Fairmont, West Virginia, the late Guy Gerard, I said, "Brother Gerard, I believe God has called me into the ministry". He said, "Brother, not everyone gets called into the ministry". I thought, well, that's that. So, I said to him, "You know, I'm working in Fairmont, West Virginia and I'm working with a gentleman that has 7 brothers and a mother and a father. That's 9 people. I'm witnessing to him and I pray to God that he gets saved so that he and his family can come to your church and we tried desperately, I witnessed to this young man and I told him

45

about how I used to be in my vices and all, thinking that if I do that he'll see how bad I was and he'll see what I am now and everybody called me John the Baptist and this and that. Nevertheless, I let the light of Jesus Christ shine in me and through me. One day this man said to me "You know something John, I appreciate what you have, you have something I don't have. You have something that the other people in this crew don't have. I'll tell you something else, I'm not as bad as you so I don't need it." I prayed for him and that was the last time I saw him. God have mercy on him.

While working with this crew, there was a gentleman by the name of Mac McDonald who lived in Boosville. Mac was a comedian. He said to the gentleman, "You people haven't been able to break John down but I will." Every lunch hour you know what John did, John read his Bible or prayed. John never took time out to eat lunch. He sought the will and the face of God. I remember one day. I went up on the scaffold and Mac went with me. Mac had just finished telling the people on the ground that he was going to tell me a dirty joke. I said to him, "I don't need your dirty joke and I don't want to hear it." He said, "Well, you'll have to hear it because your up in the air 40 feet and your going to hear it." I said, "Shame on you." I continued to paint, paint, paint. I was throwing paint every which way and the first thing you know, I had my side painted and he hadn't even started yet. He looked at me and said, "You make me sick with this religion of yours. I'm going to tell you that joke if I never see the back of my head again." He grabbed the end of the rope and he grabbed the wrong end of the rope and Mac fell through the air. He hit down on the ground. There was a scaffold down there. Mac hit the scaffold. He broke many, many bones throughout his body. He knocked all of his teeth out. He was so fearful and so shaky, that I went down on the rope to where he was at. He was moaning and groaning. I prayed for him and about that time the ambulance came. The ambulance driver said, "How many were there?" I realized they were expecting more than one to fall. I said, "I'm not the boss, I'm not going back up today." So, they took Mac to the hospital and I went along with him. I had prayer with him again. They took him into surgery. The next day I went up to see Mac. He looked at me and his face was wrapped in bandages. All I could see was his eyes and nose. He looked at me and he said, "You know John, I will never tease you again. What I need is what you have. Will you help me to find Jesus as my Savior?" I prayed for Mac McDonald and he received Jesus Christ as his Lord and Savior. Another experience working with the paint crew. I had many, many. Praise the name of the Lord.

I remember after my mother became Christian. One day she went into her bedroom and my father told me to keep my eyes open to see if she did anything strange. I watched her go into her bedroom and kneel down to her bed. She raised her hands toward Heaven and I heard her praying, saying, "Lord, save my husband. Oh God, save my son. Save my daughters and save all of your people Lord." Then she started speaking in a strange language I've never heard. I understood the Italian language quite well. It wasn't Italian. I walked away disturbed in my spirit. Then I went back to the door again. My sister Evelyn wanted to know what I was doing. I said, "I'm watching mommy because I believe she's sick, there is something wrong with her." I went back to the door again. I could see tears coming down her cheeks. She was saying, "Oh God, oh God. I know you here my prayer. I want to see my husband saved. I want to see my son and my daughter saved. I want to see our family happy Lord because all I have is turmoil, problems, troubles and tribulations. I'm not complaining because of that Lord. I do want to see my family saved." Then in my heart, which I've never forgotten, something I will always carry with me, I will always cherish this, praise the name of the Lord.

I also remember, in the 50's after I became a Christian, it seemed that I just couldn't find a job. One day I was notified that there was an opening for me. It was for an Insurance Company. I remember Brenda was so thrilled, we went to the store where my wife was working, then from there we went to the insurance company and we had to climb a flight of stairs about 20 steps. Her face was just beaming as I went up to talk to the insurance man. He said, "I'll start you out at $9,700.00 a year", and I can increase my salary according to the hours I put into my work. Then I said to him "When do I start?" He said, "Well, let's get something straight first, you are a minister aren't you?" I said, "Well, I have a mission that I take care of but I'm only there Saturday night and Sunday afternoon. Your telling me that the work with you is only 5 days a week. He said, "That's true but we'll have to have all of you,." I said, "You will have all of me." He said, "No, no, I mean we want all of you." I looked at him and I said, "You mean I'll have to give up my mission working for the Lord?" He said, "That's right." I said, "I'm sorry, I can't do that." I thanked him and walked out. We walked down the steps, as we got to the foot of the steps on the street, Brenda looked at me with her face beaming and she said, "Daddy, I'm so glad that you told him." Then I remember after I became a Christian, I started launching out with not so much the younger people but the older people. I remember starting prayer meetings in the old timers homes. I used to go to Sister Barlow's home down in Dawmont, Sister Perry's home in Dawmont, and Sister Barlow had a sister named Mary. I don't remember her last name but she was some lady. I remember I went through a very difficult time, my battery was dead in my automobile and Mary reached into her wallet and pulled out $20.00 and said, "Brother Johnny, you buy yourself a battery." I remember wanting to pay her back and she said, "No, no, I don't want your money, I want you to pray for me."

Mary, the lady that bought me the battery, shortly after that was saved. She received Christ as her Lord and Savior. I never saw anything like it. She would go to her neighbors, to her friends and relatives and she would say to them, "Don't tell me any gossip. Don't tell me anything about what's going on in the world. What I want to know is more about Jesus. He is the one I love. He is the one I want to see." Then she would say, "Read the Bible, please read the Bible to me because I want to know more about him. He is the one that saved me, he is the one that died for me." She was really something to behold. Shortly after that, Mary suffered a stroke. Her sister, Sister Barlow, called me and I drove to the hospital furiously. When I arrived, I found Mary had suffered a stroke, something similar to that of Sam Marra. Sister Barlow grabbed my arm and practically tore my sleeve off. "Please pray Brother Johnny, please pray that God will raise my sister." The Lord just didn't lay her upon my heart to do that. I said, "I can't pray that way. We need to pray that the Lord will take your sister out of this suffering and take her to glory with him. Shortly after that he did. Little did I realize that the day would come when someone would say to me "Pray, pray, pray" for someone that is dead and God will raise them from the dead.

Another thing that I want to mention, my sister Anne Conch, who was baptized in 1949, when Doris and I were, we slipped, but Anne, never. She kept on with the Lord, even to this day. She loves the Lord with all of her heart.

On Monday nights we would go to different homes and have prayer meetings. We would go to Brother Vance's home in Norwood, we would go to Locants, to Barlow's down in Dawson and that's how Barlow's sister Mary got saved. Each time we would go to these homes, the glory of God would flood our souls. From there, we went on to the mission and Brother Iquinto went with us also. The day came that the mission was really prospering. Sister Margaret DePolo said to her husband and to me, "I think that we should build a church because we should strike now while the iron is hot." We didn't. We lost a great opportunity in doing so. The Lord I guess knows what he is doing because he had greater things for me to do for him. Shortly after that in 1953 when Doris and I came to the Lord and God filled us with the Holy Spirit, my younger sister Theresa was also saved and filled with the spirit as a matter of fact, she was filled on a Thursday, Doris on a Friday, and I on a Saturday. Theresa was moving her hands in such a way that she would have you to think that she was playing an instrument. God really filled her with his spirit because her life was never the same after that. Theresa loved to dance, but after God saved her and filled her with his spirit, the only dancing she ever did was for the Lord. Then her family got saved. Praise the Lord for all of his marvelous work he's brought upon the children of men.

On March the 9th, a Wednesday night in 1960, ordinarily my mother and I would go to the Italian service in our Clarksburg church, but this Wednesday night about 9" of snow came down in just a short while and father was so thrilled that I wasn't going out on the highway in that nasty, deep snow. About 7:00 as we were sitting around our table, Jean my niece was with us, Jean, Doris, Frank, and Brenda. Mom came over in her bare feet in all that snow and said, "You better come over and see, I think your father is dead." We ran over, I ran over in my house slippers. Father was lying on the floor and I put his head against my chest and we prayed that God would restore him, that God would touch him. Father looked at me and tears streamed down his cheeks. I embraced him and I prayed again. The Lord took my father. I think that was one of the greatest blows I was ever struck after I became a Christian. It seemed that I just couldn't understand why God would do that. Until later on when I went into full time ministry, when I prayed for different people. I saw them suffering and suffering. Then I apologized to God many, many times. Knowing that he always knows what is best. Then April, that same year in 1960, my brother-in-law, Roy Lindsey, was taken to the Veterans hospital. He was very ill. They performed an operation on him. An exploratory operation. Roy came back to the Lord, he had backslid also. Then he said to Jean, my wife, and to myself, "If I go back home, I just can't live right in that environment. While he was there in the hospital he started to bleed. Blood gushed out of him like a river. Shortly after he was dead. God had taken him. Then I went back to Canonsburg again. It was about the fourth time I was in Canonsburg.

The Great Depression was on but the Bible says I have never seen the righteous forsaken, nor a seed begging bread. We had plenty. We had hogs, we had chickens, and mom always made sure that there was plenty of meat on the table. I thank God for a Godly mother and I thank God for a mother who was really concerned for her children.

There was another incident that happened. We went to the mission and I remember being in church and praying for about 6 hours. Doris didn't feel well enough to go to the mission that night. So, Jean and Evelyn and Sister Barlow and I went. God gave us four precious souls. Four people were saved. We had a glorious time, it seemed that God really blessed in that service and someone was healed and someone was filled with the spirit of God and after it was all said and done about 11:00 at night, we all started home. I remember driving Sister Barlow home, down in the mining camp and Evelyn, dropped her off, and Jean, and then I started for home. That same spirit that I felt the night when I was awakened our of my sleep and saw Lucifer in my living room. That same spirit was in the automobile. As a matter of fact it was so strong that my hair, the back of my head, stood straight up. I was praying that a car would come so that I could see if he was actually in the back of my car. I stopped the car and I though "What is this" and I rebuked him in the name of the Lord and I got back into the automobile and continued to drive, but his spirit was still in the automobile and then I remembered pleading with Jesus Christ. Just as I came across the Meadowbrook Bridge, I pleaded the blood again. It seemed like Heaven flooded my soul. The spirit of God came upon me and I started speaking in other tongues and the spell of Satan was broken and praise the name of the Lord.

In 1956, in Volga where we held our services, it was so cold that we canceled our services. Some people there from Buckhannan, West Virginia, Brother Clark's sister-in-law, who was also a minister invited us to attend a Sunday evening service in Buckhannan in which we agreed to do. The next day we attended our church service in Clarksburg where I taught the adult Sunday school class, and then in the afternoon we went up to Volga but it was too cold. We didn't hold a service. We went up to Buckhannan in Brother Clark's church. I guess that's how the Lord intended this because when we arrived there the service was starting and Brother Clark announced to the

Congregation that Brother DePolo was going to be the speaker that night. I spoke on Luke 16:19, I didn't know why but automatically that came to my mind. As I preached on this about the rich man that found himself in the gates of Hell and I wanted to hold a prayer meeting. After it was all said and done I had an altar service. There was a young lady in the back of the church. Brother Clark said to me, "You know, she's attended services here quite frequently, but I can't get her to come to the Altar. I would appreciate it Brother DePolo if you would try." So, I went back and I said, "Young lady, I don't know who you are, but I was informed by the Pastor that you attend here quite often and I'd like for you to come up and receive my Jesus as your Lord and Savior.

If you want to go to the altar, I'll be glad to sit down here and pray with you here." She looked at me very sincere and said, "Don't waste your time with me, I'm one of those that you spoke about tonight that's in the gates of Hell. That's where I am. There was a time preacher, that I was saved and filled with the spirit of God. Then I denied the Lord and I said to the Holy Spirit, "Don't you ever bother me again", and from that day to this I have never, never felt the spirit of the Lord. I attend services yes, but not to receive what you might think. I attend the services to know that I am lost forever and the only joy I get is hearing people sing because I know in Hell there will be no joy and there is no turning back because you can talk to me all night, but the spirit of the Lord has departed from me." With that I walked away, I walked to the altar and I knelt and I prayed. Then I said to Brother Clark, I said, "You know, I've tried to deal with this young lady but, I'll explain it to you later. I would like to pray for the sick." He said, "Fine, Brother DePolo, here's the oil." I asked the people to gather around the altar. There was an elderly lady there who worked at the College. She had to retire because she had suffered a heart attack and she was barely able to walk. I said to Ruth, "We are going to pray for Sister Tenny, and Sister Tenny, if you'll please come up." Her husband came with her and I remember as though it was yesterday. I anointed her with oil in the name of the Lord and the spirit of God came up upon her and she danced and she danced and the next thing I know, she's taking off running around that church and everybody clapped their hands and everybody cheered and I thought that she was taking a shortcut through the pews, but she wasn't. She was running around that building. God had miraculously healed her and the following week the same lady that had to retire because of illness went back to work. That is the power of God. Then shortly after that, a few days later one of my co-workers, my niece Jean was stricken with a severe fever. I heard about it, so, Doris, my wife, and Frank and Brenda and I went up to pray for Jean. We went up, we prayed and prayed and prayed. About 9:00 I said to Doris, "I'm going to drive you home with the children and then I'm coming back. If the fever doesn't break I'm going to wrap Jean in a blanket, because it was in the winter time, and I'm going to drive her to St. Mary's Hospital in Clarksburg." So, I drove Doris, Frank and Brenda home. But Frank said, "Dad, I want to go back with you." I said "Alright, but don't forget tomorrow is school." He said, "Alright." So, Frank and I went back. When I arrived at my sisters I said to her, "Is Jean any better?" She says, "No, her fever is just about to hit 107 degrees." I said to her, "I don't know about this but we're going to pray one more time." Jean looked at me and said, "Uncle Johnny, rebuke this devil that is trying to destroy me." God had delivered her from Rheumatic fever twice. I said, "I know where I made my mistake." My sister looked at me in amazement and said, "You've been praying." I said, "I haven't anointed her with oil. Give me the oil please." She got me the oil. I touched the oil with my index finger. I touched Jean's brow and as Frank and my sister and Jean and I prayed, God miraculously delivered her. A few seconds later after I said Amen, we opened our eyes and I said, "Well Jean, how do you feel?" She said, "Uncle Johnny, I'm beginning to perspire. The fever is broken." Shortly after that she changed clothes and her temperature was back down to normal. That my brother, my sister, is the power of God. In our lives, breaking the yoke of Satan that try to destroy us, you see the Bible says that he that is within us is greater than he that is against us. Shortly after that we went back to our meetings in Volga, West Virginia. It was there that I realized that God was bringing this thing to a close. Then about that time, my mother at 57 became very ill. We thought she was going to have a break down. I drove her to her doctor in Phillipi, West Virginia where we held our church at this time. Dr. Ernest Guy was her doctor. Dr. Guy examined her and he said to me, "Your mom is on a verge of a nervous breakdown. What's going on?" I said, "Nothing that I know of, my father is very ill." He said, "I know, I've been doctoring your father. I don't like the electrocardiogram I took of your mothers heart." I said, "What do you mean?" He said, "Well, your mothers heart has enlarged clear across her chest. It is so large that I don't think it could

59

get much larger without exploding." I said, "You didn't tell her?" He said, "No. I said, "Don't tell her because she has enough problems without that." Then I drove that same day to Buckhannan, West Virginia where I met with my dear Brother Clark, who has since gone to be with the Lord, I said to him, "Brother Clark, my mother is ill in the hospital and God has laid on my heart to drive up after you. You and I are going to go back to Phillipi, West Virginia and we are going to pray." He said, "Brother DePolo, that is fine with me." So, I drove to Phillipi, West Virginia from Buckhannan. Brother Clark never opened his eyes. He continued speaking in tongues and praising the Lord. The spirit of the Lord was in that automobile. When we arrived at the hospital we went up to my mothers room and I said to her, "Mom, this is Brother Clark, the gentleman from Buckhannan, West Virginia. He is the minister from Buckhannan." Mom said she was glad to meet him and I said, "Well, the reason I left here a while ago and I went to Buckhannan is because Brother Clark and I are going to anoint you with oil and we're going to pray for you." So, we anointed her with oil and we prayed. Brother Clark prayed and I prayed and then Brother Clark prayed again. The spirit of the Lord came upon my mother and we left. I drove Brother Clark home and after that I went home. The next day we went to visit my mother and she was feeling much, much better. I said to Dr. Guy, I said, "Dr. Guy, how is my mother?" He said, "Well, she is a little bit better but I'm not going to discharge her until the later part of the week." I said, "Fine." The amazing thing about all of this is that a few days after that mom was discharged from the hospital and then I drove her home and then father became ill and I drove father to the hospital. Then Dr. Guy said to me about my father, "Your father could leave this world as fast as you blink your eyes." I've known this for awhile because he told me that about 7 years before and I said, "Dr. Guy, please don't say anything to my father because I don't think he could take it. Then he said to me, "What I want you to do tomorrow when you come up, because I know you come up to visit your daddy daily, I want you to bring your mother." So I brought mother and mother brought some rolls that she made for Dr. Guy because she thought the world of this man. Then he said to me, "I don't know why, but I have a feeling, I watched your mother get out of your automobile and walk up those steps, I want to take another Cardiogram." I said, "That's fine with me, because the U&W that my father belongs to has the best insurance in the world." He said, "No, the money is not the issue here,

I thing the world of your mom and dad and I think the world of you. I don't know, a person that has a heart as bad and enlarged as she did, I just don't know. Things just don't add up here." So, he took a Cardiogram, and he took a second one and then he said, "You know, I've never seen it happen before, but I have the proof that your mothers heart was healed. She no longer has an enlarged heart." My brother, my sister, that is the power of God that is manifested in our hearts and in our lives. It seemed that I spend most of my time just in the hospital. Mrs. Spores called and informed me that her husband was in the hospital. Mrs. Spores called and informed me that her husband was in the hospital. And of all places, Buchannan, West Virginia. I went up to visit with him and he was the gentleman that was healed of Brights disease. I said to him, "Brother Spores, how are you?" He was reluctant to speak about his illness. I prayed with him and I could hear a lady across the hall from his room, she was crying and was agonizing. I went over and I said, "May I help you?" She said, "I don't think you can. The doctors informed me that my husband is very, very bad and I'm afraid he's going to leave this world and he's not saved." I said to him, "Sir, you need Jesus Christ as your Lord and Savior. You need to surrender your heart and your life to him. He is able to save your soul and heal your body." He looked at me and grinned. He said, "What do you want me to do?" I said, "You repeat after me." He repeated the sinner prayer. "Jesus I'm a sinner, save me by your power and make me what you would have me to be and Jesus I surrender my life completely to you." I didn't add that on, he did. After it was all said and done the husband and wife both gave their hearts to the Lord. Two days later, I went up to visit Brother Spores and I said to him, "How is the gentleman across the way?" He said, "Didn't anybody tell you?" I said, "Tell me what?" He said, "Didn't anybody tell you that the next day the doctors examined him and they didn't find anymore heart trouble. They couldn't find anything wrong with the man and he was discharged from this hospital." The reason I'm saying this is to show and to prove and to show you and tell the world what a great God we serve. How he is able to do anything. How he is able to do exceedingly and abundantly of all that which we think or even ask. So I thank God that we serve a God who is able to undertake a God that is able to deliver, a God that is able to set us free from all sickness and all disease and make us what he wants us to be. Praise the name of the Lord.

In our mission we had a young lad, the first time we met him, Johnny was about 10 years of age. Johnny Canter was his name. Johnny was born blind. Johnny attended the school for the blind and Rominey, West Virginia, where he learned to read Braille. God used this young man to play the piano. He could sit with his back to the piano and play Amazing Grace like nobody else. Johnny really loved the Lord and I remember when Johnny was baptized he was very discouraged and very disappointed. Then he looked at my wife and said, "I'm so hurt, I thought for sure when I came up out of the water I was going to see my mother to see what she looked like." Doris said to him, "Johnny, one day when we all get to Heaven your mother will get there also and you'll be able to see what she looks like." Johnny, really loved the Lord, he attended Canonsburg, probably two years later in '62 or '63, we were informed by a lady that knew Johnny Canter, he became very ill and he was having convulsions, even at the time he was coming to our services, and he was admitted to St. Mary's hospital in Clarksburg, West Virginia. He was very, very ill. The nurses felt so bad for him. They realized he was blind. I guess he was in his last hour before the Lord would take him home to Glory. As the story goes, there were two Catholic nurses that told this, they said that they didn't want to see him suffer so they turned the light out in his room and they went out into the hallway. As they stood out there they kept conversing and they realized that it was about time that Johnny would leave this world. All of a sudden they looked at the bottom of the door and they saw a light in there. They opened the door and they said that there was a glow around his bed and the Angels had come to take Johnny home. They even heard Angelic singing. Praise the name of the Lord. These ladies that didn't know a thing about the Lord, but they knew that God had come to take Johnny home.

Johnny had a sister by the name of Betty. Betty was a junior in highschool. I believe that Betty wore the thickest glasses that I have ever seen. Her eyes were so terrible that without her glasses she couldn't recognize her mother or anyone else. I remember one evening when Betty came to our service. She looked at me and she said, "Reverend DePolo, I want you to pray that God will heal my eyes. They are getting worse. Soon, if God doesn't undertake and do something I'm going to be like my brother Johnny, blind." We felt so bad, we anointed her with oil. That name which is above every name and the power of God came down upon her. She removed her glasses and she commenced to cry and then she looked at my Bible and she said she could read it without her glasses. She read other peoples Bibles and the Psalm book and she was so thrilled. She would no longer have to worry about going blind. Then after we dropped Betty, John, and her mother off, they went into the house and Betty realized one thing, that they lived in a one bedroom house. There were 14 in the family. She thought, well if I put my glasses up on the mantle, perhaps one of my brothers or sisters will knock them off. Well, maybe I'll put my glasses in the dresser drawer, but what if one of my brothers or sisters go in the dresser drawer and drops them and steps on them. Then what, what if I need them again. I know the safest place for my glasses. To put them on my face. So, Betty put her glasses on her face and went to sleep. The next morning when she woke up she removed her glasses to prove to her mother and the others that she could read. She was as blind as ever. She couldn't see without her glasses. I remember that next week when they come to the meeting, we picked her up and first thing she said to me was, "Brother Johnny, your going to have to pray for me." I said, "Betty, what did you do?" Then she told me the story. We prayed for her and we anointed her with oil, but nothing happened. The last time I saw

Betty, she was still wearing those glasses and that was 31-32 years ago.

In 1958, my sister Mary and I drove Frank to Philadelphia to Eastern Bible Institute. We stopped off in Philadelphia to visit with my cousin Joe Audia. They drove us down to the college. We came back, and Frank, Joe and Frank Doncolonk and I, we left Mary at Joe's house, and we went down to Father Devines place in Philadelphia. We were there a short while and there was a man with a crew cut, we asked him questions about Father Devine. He pointed out Father Devine's white angel, a young lady all dressed in white, and we questioned him about Father Devine. Although we didn't get to see Father Devine. He pointed out another man, he made him out to be Father Devine. He could have been. We felt and sensed the demon spirits from the world beneath because we had chills and goose bumps. My two cousins, who were both Catholics, looked at me and they said, "John, what is that odd feeling. What is that/" I had goose bumps while we were in there, and we tried to explain to them about this man called Father Devine and his group of worshipers he had with him. I never saw anything like that, I never felt anything like that until the time we had the encounter with the demons with Harold

67

Hall. Then we had the same thing over and over again. We drove Frank to the Bible College in Philadelphia and then we left Frank there and then Mary and I drove to Baltimore to visit with my sister Rose and we waited there 2 days hoping against hope that Frank would call and say that he would want to come home. Then from there we returned home to Meadowbrook. My father was so brokenhearted. He said, "Why did you leave him in Philadelphia?"

In 1964, our daughter Brenda married into the family of the founder of our Washington, PA church, Br. Saverio Marasco. His eldest son James had a son, also named James like his father, and Brenda was married in May, 1964. Their first son born in 1966 lived only one day and the Lord took him to heaven. The Lord then gave them another beautiful son in 1967, James Brent. In 1968, again Brenda and Jimmy were blessed with a beautiful baby girl, Larissa Lyn.

On Tuesday, October 1, 1964, the day before I bought a new car, a new Mercury, I found myself at a carwash of all places with a new car. Not knowing why or understanding why the Lord led me there. A man by the name of Dominic Falconi, the owner of the carwash, immediately starting spraying water on my car. I said, "Why are you doing that, I have a new automobile?" He said, "Well, there is bound to be some dust on it, I'm going to wipe it too." I said, "I'm Pastor DePolo and your name is?" He said, "Dominic Falconi. My brother and I own half of Washington County." I said, "I'm pleased to meet you, but I think you need the Lord, don't you?" He looked at me with tears streaming down his cheek and he said, "Yes, I do." I said, "If you mean what you say, jump in my automobile." Lo and behold I marveled, the man opened the door on the passenger side, he jumped in and said, "Let's go." Our church in Canonsburg was only a few blocks away on Payne Place. I drove the car to Payne Place and he got out of the car before I did. We went into the church and he knelt to pray and he prayed in this fashion: "God forgive me for stealing this and God forgive me for cheating that man", and so on. I said, "Dominic, we don't do that. We ask the Lord to forgive us our faults and our failures our shortcomings and sins and it's all wrapped up in a nut shell and he forgives us." He said, "You'll have to each me how to do that." So I did, I said, "Now you ask Jesus to come into your heart and into your life." He did. I said, "Aren't you thrilled that you're saved?" He said, "Yes, I am." I looked at him and I said, "Dominic, God loves you." The man began to weep and he looked at me and he said, "You don't know why you came to my place do you?" I said, "No, I don't." He said, "For the simple reason I was all set to take my life and here is the 38 pistol I was going to do it with." He handed the gun to me. I said, "I don't want it. You take it.and destroy it. Dominic, don't you ever think of that again. Why would you do such a thing?" He said, "I have a very close friend and he wanted to borrow $12,000.00 and instead of going to a notary and having it notarized, I didn't do that because word of mouth to me means everything, and after 2 years this friend of mine said that I didn't loan him any money. He said he didn't owe me any money. My brother knew about it and he harassed me. Caesar harassed me. He was as good as his name Caesar, believe you me because I know the man. I was so upset with myself and with my brother, I thought I would end it all right at this carwash at 11:00, and you showed up at 10:45. God has spared my life." I was there with the man, Caesar Falconi, I spoke to him later about his soul, I was there with Dominic the night the Lord was taking him home. I said, "Dominic, you hold on with all that your worth because God is going to see you through." He looked at me and said, "Preacher, I'm glad you came to that carwash. Now, I can rest in peace knowing that I'm going home to be with the Lord." Shortly after that, Dominic Falconi graduated. He went to be with the Lord Jesus Christ.

October 19, Joe Angelillo was stricken with what we might call discouragement with the devil. His wife Lucy had gone to California to visit with her grandson who was very ill and she overstayed her stay out there, Joe was very, very concerned about it and lo and behold he got so discouraged he went to the doctor and the doctor couldn't do a thing for him. Doctor Berman said, "We're going to have to send you to a Psychiatrist and I hope and pray that he can help you because I can't. I would like to but there is no need for you to come back to my office. You need to go to a mental hospital." It was on a Saturday morning, I went to the Angelillo's home and the son-in-law and daughter were living upstairs and I called them to come down. They came down, Joe and Lucy. Tony and Jimmy and I held hands and lo and behold God came down and healed Joe within a twinkle of an eye. You see, my God can do anything, anything but fail. God wants to deliver us, God wants to move upon us and we as Christians are sitting back instead of coming forward and having the Lord Jesus Christ move upon us and quicken us with the power of his Holy Spirit. God wants to heal, God wants to save, God wants to move into the hearts and the lives of his people, but seemingly we are all sitting back and we want the Lord to feed us at times, and we want him to give us the bottle at times, but my God can do anything and everything and he's not going to do that. I have in my notes that on Thursday, October 15, 1964, I bought Phillip (our first grandson) his first football. Then Wednesday, March 24, 1965, Andy Jr. was taken to the Washington Hospital. This young man was 27 years of age. I never met him before. I went up and Sam introduced me to Andy. The doctor said that Andy had double Pneumonia. I realized as they continued to run tests on Andy Jr. that it wasn't double Pneumonia, he was to be discharged on a Friday and the doctor said, "You know we're going to keep you over. We found something that we are just not pleased with." Andy wanted to know what it was. The doctor said to the father that he had found a spider like form that has taken the upper part of his extremities. His lungs and even touching his heart and they believed it was cancer. The doctor said, "I'm not sure but we'll have to operate one Monday morning." So, that night, it was on a Saturday night, Andy Sr. said to me, "I'd like to ask you questions about the Bible DePolo." I said, "Andy, I will answer your question with the Bible." After awhile, he got so irritated with the answers the

Bible gave me. He said, "You take that Bible and you can shove it and go with it." On a Monday morning at 6:30, Sam and I went up to pray for Andy Jr. before they took him up to surgery. It's amazing because Andy had surgery, they removed nothing. I met the doctor on the elevator and I said to him, "Dr. what about Andy Jr." He said, "That's confidential, I can't reveal that to you." I said, "I'm his Pastor and the family will be asking me." He said, "Well, don't let him know because he is running scared and why wouldn't he, 27 years of age and only has 3 months to live. The longest I'll give him is 6 months." When Andy Sr. heard that, Sam and I left the hospital, we went down to our home on Jefferson Avenue. As we entered the door, Doris said, "Where have you been, I've been trying to contact you. Andy Mac has been trying to call, Andy tried to call, Mary Mac tried to call, what is the problem?" I said, "Andy Jr. has cancer. The doctor said he'll live 3 months, 6 months at the longest. That is why Andy is so upset." She said, "Andy wants you." I said, "Why would he want me after the way he treated me last night." She said, "His wife said he is on his knees crying out to God and God won't save him." I Said to Sam, "Let's go out and see." Sam said, "She is lying. Andy Mac Sr. can not kneel." I said, "Sam, if he can't kneel then it means he is lying, but if we go out there and he is on his knees then what do we day. She said, "Then I'll believe it." So, we went out and knocked on the door and lo and behold, from Andy's kitchen door you can look straight into the bedroom, when she opened the door Andy was on his knees. Sam said, "Now I believe it." Now, I'm trying to get back at Andy Sr. You know that caliber sometime gets a little rock and a little hard and I said, "I know what your looking for Mr. Mac. You thought that because Andy was coming to the Lord Jesus Christ that the bells were going to sound, the angels were going to ring chimes and they were going to acknowledge that Andy Mac Sr. was coming to the Lord." He said, "Yes, how did you know all that?" I said, "God does not operate that way brother. The bible says that you are saved by grace through faith. Put your faith in the Lord Jesus Christ and you've already acknowledged that, your faith in Heaven. He saved you and you don't realize it." So, we prayed with him and we went on our way. Andy Mac Sr. got genuinely saved and not only did Andy Mac Sr. get saved but his wife, his daughter-in-law, his sister, they were all saved. They all started coming to the church and we realized that Andy Jr. had been told, the doctor told the family not him, that his stay on earth would be very brief. Three months to 6 months at the longest. We started to have special prayer meetings in our church in Washington. I was still Pastoring 2 churches. The church in Washington and the church in Canonsburg. God is blessing both churches. The both of them were pretty well filled. We were trying to start a building fund to start building a new church in the Washington Community. People just couldn't believe it, what are these people trying to do. They are trying to build a new church and they just can't do it. They don't have the collateral, they don't have this and they don't have that. But, they failed to realize that God was on the throne and God was moving and God wanted to do these great and mighty things for his people. So, we started praying for Andy and he started going to Pittsburgh taking his treatments. One day, Doris and I drove Mary, his wife, over to pick up her husband and bring him home and the doctor in Pittsburgh looked at Andy and said, "Are you Andy Mac Jr.?" Andy said, "Yes I am, am I worse?" He said, "Worse, no, look at all these people in my office, they are all dying with cancer. But you, I don't know, but God has given you back your life." So, Andy Jr. Left there knowing and realizing that God healed his body.

Sunday, July 25, 1965, we bought our lots for our new church and we were ready to build now because God is really blessing the

Washington church, we had a ground breaking ceremony. Reverend Corsini spoke. What had happened was that just as we were ready to start our services outside the rain clouds came overhead. Reverend Corsini said, Brother DePolo it is going to rain." I said, "It is not going to rain, God has blessed us and God is going to keep that rain away from here until the service is over." God honored my faith, because the rain did not come until the service was over. So, we broke ground and greater things were yet to come for the Washington church. Then one day somebody told me about a young man by the name of Kenneth Guy who had 58 blood transfusions in the Washington Hospital. His stomach was perforated and the doctors said there was nothing they could do for him. Guy had a loving mother who is deceased now, his mother would say to me, "Please pray for Guy, I know that the doctors can't help. I understand that you know how to get a hold of God and that you people know how to pray." We prayed for Guy, and we kept praying for Guy. One day lo and behold, when I went up to visit Guy, Kenneth Guy was dressed ready to go home. The doctor said, "We cannot find a perforated stomach any longer. We do not know what has taken plea but one thing we do know is that God has blessed you and God has done something."

Sunday, October 16, 1965, I was asked to visit a gentleman by the name of Amos Behanna. Amos had suffered a heart attack. Doctor Badiali was his doctor. I went up to pray for Amos. After I prayed Amos looked at me and said, "Let me see your hands." I said, "Why do you ask to see my hands?" He said, "Because when you prayed, somebody shocked me." I said, "I did not." I showed him the palms of my hands and he said, "You know those little gadgets that you put in your hand when you shake people's hands? He said, I got a shock like that." I said, "Well, it wasn't me." Dr. Badiali came in and Amos said, "You know, I believe God healed me." Dr. Badiali took his stethoscope off and put it in to operation and checked Amos's heart and he said, "No, it's still irregular. Where did you get this healing bit?" He said, "Well, Pastor DePolo prayed for me." Dr. Badiali looked at me and said, "Oh, that fellow. No, he didn't heal you." Amos said, "I didn't say he healed me but, I thought I got healed and he didn't say anything." So, we went back the next day and Amos said, "Check me out, I'm pretty sure God healed me." He said, "No, you still have that irregular heartbeat Amos. I was going to check you anyway. You tell that minister that you're not healed." The third day, lo and behold, it had dawned on Amos what had happened, because the late Jim Mazzie use to say to me that Amos coughed so long and so loud that if Emphysema would attack him and he would cough so hard that he would break ribs. He said to Dr. Badiali, "Check my lungs." He checked his lungs and sent him down to x-ray and brought him back up and said, "Amos, if I had that kind of medicine I'd become a billionaire over night." We prayed that God would heal his heart, but God healed his Emphysema. You see, we prayed one way but God healed another. But we'll take it any way. Amos Behanna was never ever again bothered by emphysema. Even to the day he was hit with an automobile and passed away he was never bothered with emphysema. So, you see, God does hear and God does answer prayer.

Doris and I were ready to go to Clarksburg, West Virginia to visit with my mother and her family in Lumberport, West Virginia. This was also in 1966, we received a phone call from Joanne Loasey telling us that her neighbor by the name of Joe Bruckner was shot by his wife. I went to visit him while Doris stayed in the car. This was Friday, May 12, 1966. We prayed for him but Joe was in a coma. We went to West Virginia and came back that same night. That next morning I went up to visit Joe and I prayed with him again. This time he was no longer comatosed. He looked at me and he said, "You prayed for me yesterday didn't you." I said, "Yes." He said, "I heard you. I want to receive Jesus as my Lord and Savior." The doctor said he cannot live, where the bullet entered his body, it was too close to his heart. But, we prayed that Joe give his heart to the Lord. Three days later he was discharged from the hospital and this was 1966 and as far as I know 1992, I heard from Joe in 1990 and he is fine and doing well, which tells me God can do exceedingly and abundantly above that which we ask or even think. One of my parishioners was in the hospital. Sister Virginia Chicone. She was at the hospital on the sixth floor. Of all things when I went up to visit her I noticed the room she was in was 666. I said to her, "Sister Chicone, do you know what room they put you in?" She said, "No honey." I said, "You're in room 666." Sister Chicone screamed for the nurse. The nurse come running and she said, "Is their something wrong?" She said, "Yes, yes, take me out of this room. I don't want to be in the room 666. You put me in another room." The nurse put me in another room and said, "You did this didn't you?" I had no answer because I wanted to see Sister Chicone's reaction. Thursday, July 23, 1964, Sister Manfreede called me while we were still living in Canonsburg. She called and said that her daughter Rose had suffered a facial paralysis and some type of a stroke and asked if I could come and pray for her. I said, "Sister Manfreede, I'm on my way to the Washington church to the Italian service which starts at 7:00 and I'll be at your place at 6:30. Lo and behold, they lived on Jefferson Avenue and as we came to Washington from Canonsburg July 23, 1964, right in her parking lot I anointed her daughter Rose Ferguson with oil in the name of the Lord and I offered up the prayer of faith. Doris and I went on to the service and I said to Sister Manfreede, "I would like to know what happens, if they admit your daughter or if they take her back home." Sister Manfreede was so gracious because on the way home she stopped at the church. She wanted me to know firsthand that the doctors said her daughter had suffered a stroke and as they were examining her and all of the paralysis had left. They could not find a trace of it. She stood up and testified. She said, "I know that God has healed my daughter."

Sunday, October 16, 1966, after we moved to Washington, our first service in the new church, we had a full house. In that same year, 1966, Don Swaggert, a gentleman who I was told about was in the hospital. He was in an automobile accident and he had suffered a stroke. Each day, he was in a coma, I'd go in and pray with him. After about the 35th day I went in to pray for Don Swaggert, his father was there. His father said, "You and I don't believe the same. I'm an Episcopalian. In your belief, do you believe that my son will live again?" I said "Yes, I do. If I didn't think so I wouldn't waste my time nor God's either." I happened to be there on the 68th day when Don Swaggert come out of his coma. The nurse screamed and yelled. She said, "Look, his body is moving, his body is moving." Don opened his eyes and looked at me and said, "Pastor, you're Pastor DePolo, I heard you pray every time that you come in here. I heard your conversation with my daddy and I'm glad that you put him in his place." Don Swaggert was delivered from the comatose condition. He received Jesus Christ as his Lord and Savior and the Lord raised him up. That was in 1966, in 1990 Don Swaggert got married and he married a lady whom we all know, Nancy Chechinski.

Sunday, June 26, 1966 at 4:00 a.m., Sam Mazzie called me and said, "We need to go over and pray for Ronnie Hartley." He was dying and probably would have been dead before we arrived. He said, "I will meet you at the bottom of the hill and we'll go over in your automobile. Sam and I drove through Mt. Lebanon on Rt. 19 (there was no Rt. 79 then), I was going 85 miles an hour. What I didn't know then was what I know now, regardless of who is ill or who your going to visit, if the police catch you speeding your going to pay a fine. I thought it was legitimate because he was dying and it was an emergency call. But, there are no emergency calls for the Pastors or the Preachers. Only for those that the police choose to protect. Nevertheless, we didn't get caught. The man tried to stop us but he couldn't, we were going too fast for him. Then we arrived at the hospital. We went in and the lady had already covered him over. Lizy was there, his mother, and she said to Sam and to me, "Please pray, pray, pray, I know he is dead but God is able to bring him back." We prayed for Ronnie Hartley, Ricky Hartley rather and God touched him. The sheet started to move and the nurse said, "I don't know what's going on." I said, "I believe God is bringing the young man back." It was 5:30 a.m. and when she removed she ran to the phone and said, "Call the doctor. His pupils are dilating. This young man that you said was dead, is alive again." The doctor said, "I don't believe it, what have you been drinking?" She said, "I've been drinking nothing but water." We arrived back home around 7:10. We went to church. What a miracle. When we told about that miracle,

God blessed in that service. I can still see it. The following Wednesday morning prayer service is the one I would like to emphasize, there were about 30 of us. Several of the men worked at Jessop Steel, every Wednesday morning we had a 10:00 a.m. morning prayer service and just as we were concluding the prayer service at 11:15-11:20, I noticed to my left, over toward the houses, I set my Bible down, I placed it next to the pew on the left, and I saw a huge being so tall and so beautifully white and I told the folk what I had seen and what I was seeing. The power of God had come down and we were there until 3:30 in the afternoon, raising and worshiping the Lord. Jean Harris saw what was happening, so she ran to her mothers house and picked up her sister, Mildred Levinson. Mildred came in and started playing the piano. I never in my life heard music like that. God had inspired that girls fingers and she played like an Angelic being. The spirit of the Lord was in that place and God moved in a miraculous way and everyone that was there, I'm sure will never forget it. That following Sunday, in1966, Sunday night, Jean Harris had an asthma attack. She was unable to come to the church. I thought it was very strange for Jean Harris to not come to the church. Jean Harris really loves the Lord and she is a wonderful Christian. After the service I said to my wife, we lived on Jefferson Avenue, "I'm going out to pray for Jean Harris." As I entered my automobile, there was a beautiful fragrance in the automobile. When I drove to the Harris home, which is about a half mile away, the fragrance was still there. I got out of the car and the fragrance was still with me. I went into the house and the fragrance was there. Jean Harris can still say that she smelled that fragrance. I said to her, she was laying in her chair, "Jean, how do you feel?" She said, "I can hardly breathe." I said to her husband, "We're going to anoint your wife with oil in the name of the Lord and we're going to pray for her." We did just that, and God's power came down and healed Jean Harris in 1966. This is 1992 and I've never heard Jean Harris complain about an Asthma attack again. Praise the name of the Lord. Isn't he our God, isn't he wonderful? Yes, and he want's us to love him and serve him and live for him all the days of our lives. Then that same year in 1966, which was a very notable year, after our service in Canonsburg, I'm still Pastoring the two churches, Andy Jr., Andy Sr., Jack Shepard, Doris and I went to the Paul Pierson's home to anoint Paul Pierson with oil because he was in a coma. Each one of us took turns praying for him. We anointed him with oil in the name of the Lord Jesus Christ and the

Bible says then the prayer faith shall heal the sick. As we were praying, Jack Shepard was on my left side, my wife was on my right side, I saw Paul Pierson start to move. Jack Shepard jumped to his feet. He was ready to go through the door. Shortly after, Paul Pierson sat up on the couch, he went to the table and he started to eat. He said, "You know, I'm really hungry." Wasn't that just like our God. Praise his Holy name. That's not all. God has used us because God is always looking for vessels, it is not me, I or my, it's Jesus Christ that lives with us. He's always looking for vessels that he can use. So, on Monday, March 28, 1966, Lee Mazzie was ill. Her heart was fluttering. Andy Sr., Andy Jr., Jack Shepard, Doris, Sam, Dolly and Debbie Tallerico were there. We prayed for over two hours and I said to our Brother Sam after we prayed our throats were so dry, I was still drinking coffee at that time which was shortly after, I said to Sam, "Put on some coffee, we could all enjoy a good cup of coffee." While Sam put the coffee on, Doris picked up the Bible and Doris started reading from Psalm 121. This is what Doris read, "I will lift up to the hills from whence cometh my help. My help cometh from the Lord which made Heaven and Earth. He will not suffer thy foot to be moved, he that keepeth they would not slumber. Behold he that

85

keepeth shall neither slumber or sleep. The Lord is thy keeper, the Lord is thy shade upon thy right hand. The sun shall not smite the by day or the moon by night. The Lord shall preserve thy going out and thy coming in from this time forth even for ever more." Shortly after Doris read that she yelled out, she said, "God has healed thee." She ran into the kitchen into the bedroom and lo and behold, Lee was sitting up in bed. Her blouse was no longer moving from the rapid heartbeat and after awhile, she got out of bed and moving the strangest thing happened, Mary Mac Jr. called her husband Andy and she said, "Do you know Andy, while you were praying for Lee I can tell you the type of gown she had on because God showed me this in the vision. She had a pink nightgown on and I could tell you what happened because Jesus Christ was here and he was revealing to me step by step. The spirit of the Lord came upon her and she starts speaking in the most marvelous tongues that I've ever heard.

April 27, 1967, I was asked to visit Sister Hickman at the Washington Hospital. She had suffered a heart attack, I went up to pray for her on a Thursday the 27th. I prayed for a lady in the room with her who was blind. Doris and I left for Detroit, Michigan for the district meeting. We were there Thursday, Friday, and Saturday and we returned home on Saturday night. I couldn't wait to visit Sister Hickman. When I arrived she was ready to go home. God had healed her from the first time we prayed. She said the pain was gone. They kept running tests on her because the problem was solved. Because Jesus Christ is the problem solver. The other lady that was in the room with her, her name was Stella, and Sister Pearl Hickman said to me, "God is so good." She looked at Stella and she said, "Dear, will you tell the Pastor what color tie he has on." The lady actually floored me when she said, "He has a gray and red striped tie on." God had opened her eyes. Praise the name of the Lord. Shortly after that, I had an appointment with Dr. Sulkowski, my dentist. His wife called me and she said he'd have to cancel the appointment because my appointment was the next day. Dr. Sulkowski has been ill and he's been taking medicine and nothing seems to help. He is taking so much medication that they'll probably have to put him in the hospital and run tests on him. I said to his wife Josephine, "Josephine, may I speak to the doctor?" She said, "Surely." So, Dr. Sulkowski came to the phone and I prayed a very short and simple prayer. It's not the long prayer that God answers, it's not the short prayer that God answers, but it's the prayer that comes from the heart. If Peter prayed a long prayer, he would have drowned. But, he said, "Lord Jesus, help me." I prayed Lord Jesus, I don't know what Dr. Sulkowski's problem is, but I know that your the problem solver. I pray in your mighty name that you will heal him. So we hung up our phone. Five minutes later, Dr. Sulkowski calls me and he says, "Reverend, you can come tomorrow." His wife said to me, "He's jumping around because of the way he feels. He's jumping around like he's in his 20's." He was in his 60's. Dr. Sulkowski told everyone about the marvelous healing that he received. His doctor friends, his prodigies, they all laughed at him and made fun of him, but never the less Jesus Christ had healed Dr. Sulkowski. You see, Jesus Christ healed Dr. Sulkowski, Jesus Christ wants to heal you. He wants to move in your life. The greatest healing from you sins, S-I-N-S, from your sins. Jesus Christ came to set the captive free, he came that you and I might have light and light more above.

In Isaiah, Chapter 61, the spirit of the Lord God is upon me because the Lord anointed me to preach good tidings unto the meek. He has sent me to bind up the broken hearted. To proclaim liberty of locaptis, and the opening of the prison of them that are bound and the acceptable year of the Lord and the day of vengeance of our God. To comfort all that mourn. Notice to a point unto them that morn and mine to give unto them beauty for ashes. The oil of joyful warning that God prays for the spirit of heaviness. That joyful warning that God prays for the spirit of heaviness. That they might be called trees of righteous. The planting of the Lord that he might be glorified. You may say to me, "But, preacher that's Old Testament scripture." Now turn to Luke 4, Chapter 4 vs. 18. "The spirit of the Lord is upon me because he had anointed me to preach the gospel of the poor. He has sent me to heal the broken hearted to preach the libs of baptism to recover sights of the blind. To set up liberty, them that are bruised, to preach septile year of the Lord." He closed the book and he gave it again to the minister and sat down and the eyes of all them that were in synagogue were fasted on him. He began to say unto them, this day is this scripture fulfilled in your ears.

The same year 1967, Sam Muzzie said to me, "I understand that Robin Johnson needs a healing. Her daddy said to me that they found a lump on her breast." So, I said to Sam, "Let's go to her house and pray." This was after Wednesday morning prayer meeting. Just as we arrived, the bus arrived. Her mother said, "I'm sorry but I'll have to put her in the automobile and take her to the doctor because they are waiting to do a biopsy." So, Sam and I said at the same time we want to anoint her with oil and then you can take her. We anointed her with oil in the name of the Lord Jesus Christ. By the time they arrived at the doctors office, he looked at one breast and he couldn't find a lump and he looked at the other and he couldn't find anything. He said, "I don't know what's going on but I can find nothing." Praise is he unto be our God. Isn't God able to do all things and doesn't he do them well when we least expect it. Praise his Holy Spirit.

In June, 1968, Brother Areno, Lewis Areno called me to pray for his grandson Jimmy Waner with a tumor on his arm. The doctor wanted to operate but they had to get the fathers consent and Jim was in the service. He kept the family up night and day crying for three nights and three days. After we anointed him with oil the Lord removed the tumor and the doctors couldn't find it. I give God all the glory. Praise Jesus, Praise his Holy and Matchless name. As I look at the ocean I realize how great God is. He has the whole world in the palm of his hand. At times we think that God is just too small to answer us, but I want you to know that my God is big.

May, 1968, Janet Reese was having problems and the doctors realized that it was nerve in her back and she was expecting a child.

Big with child. The doctors said, "Well there is nothing we can do about it now, we are going to have to fit you for a brace." She called me one night and she said, "Brother DePolo, will you please pray for me. I'm having so much discomfort and so much pain." Before we finished praying she said, "The pain is gone." She went back to the doctor and the doctor said, "I don't know what's happened but you don't need the brace." Praise His Holy name. Praise the name of the Lord who shall be glorified now and forever. The brace was made, but she didn't need it. Thanks to our God.

May 15, 1968, our niece Jean who is very close to me, was expecting a child. She only weighted about 80 pounds and 9 months pregnant. Her mother was staying at our house. The doctor said he would have to induce labor. We prayed and we got a hold of God and God got a hold of us and we were sure they wouldn't have to do any such thing. The next morning, bright and early, Jean went into labor without any inducement from the doctor. She had a beautiful baby boy. He weighed 6 pounds. His name is Tim. We give God all the glory because it was a healthy boy. It just had to be God because Jean couldn't eat and there was nothing the doctors could do. It had to be God. God gave her a beautiful young boy. A healthy young man. We had a write up about this in our Vista Magazine, our organizational paper about how god performed this mighty miracle in the life of my niece. Jean and her husband John also have a beautiful daughter, her name is Lisa.

In September, 1967, it was my final week at the Canonsburg church. I gave them 2 weeks notice and I left graciously because now I can work in one church. I thank God for the years that he gave me with those people down there. When I left, Canonsburg had a full church and it's amazing the young man that was healed of cancer became the Pastor of the Canonsburg church. Andy Mac Jr. A young man who was as close to me as my own son. I thank God that I have a son that is also in the ministry. He is one of the best Bible teachers that I have ever heard teach He is a great preacher. His name is Frank. Frank didn't want to get involved with Andy Mac Jr., because he along with all the others believed that Andy was going to die within the 3-6 months. Then he and Andy became as close as brothers. My God is able to do all things and he does them so beautifully.

I was so busy when I Pastored both churches. My services, Monday night bible study in the Washington church, Tuesday prayer meeting in the Canonsburg church, Wednesday prayer service at 10:00 in the

Washington church. Wednesday night 7:30 the mid-week Washington church, Friday prayer service in Washington, Sunday morning at 9:30 the service in the Canonsburg church, Sunday at 11:00 the service in the Washington church and then Sunday night at 7:30 the service in the Canonsburg church. I believe that is why God blessed my ministry.

Sunday night, December 6, 1970, two young men were saved in the evening service. Doris, my wife, led Steve Markham to the Lord while I was teaching the young people downstairs. When I came up I saw the young man crying. He told me that Doris had prayed with him. After the service, he started to leave and he said to me, "I need more from the Lord." I invited him to come back to the altar, which he did. God filled him with his Holy Spirit. Great revival broke out in our church. It spread to the churches in and around Washington and Pennsylvania.

Sunday December 13, Sam Mazzie and I went to the hospital to visit Reverend Young. He refused prayer. The gentleman in the next room was healed after we prayed for him. Our New Years Eve service started about 10:30 p.m. Over 100 people attended. We prayed until 3:00 a.m. in the morning. This is revival such as we've never seen before. People are being filled with the spirit in every service. Sick bodies are being healed and demon's were being cast out in the mighty name of Jesus. Two young ladies received the baptism after 1:30 a.m. Sunday, January 3, 1971, we had four filled with the spirit and the young man delivered from demons. God is really moving by his spirit.

Sunday, January 24, in the evening service five were filled with the spirit and two young men were delivered from demon's. God gave us the victory. We came home after 11:00 p.m.

Tuesday, February 9, we went to visit Brother Groves, Sam Mazzie and I. He was very angry with us. Brother Goves had fallen from his roof onto his head and he was critical. We prayed for him and he said the Lord was showing him Heaven. We anointed him with oil and the Lord said to him he'll have to go back. I must honor the faith in my service. He lived for 15 years and when the Lord called him home, Brother Groves was 94 years young.

Friday, July 30, 1970, Milly Crouse called me at the beauty shop. The shop that my daughter owned where my wife was working I went to pick up my wife. She wanted us to stop at her home on our way home. We did. We met a Mr. Zimmerman from Canada who was hurting very bad from a ruptured disk. We anointed him with oil and left. After we prayed the prayer of faith, Saturday, October 23, we were invited to the Johnson's home for dinner. They said they had a surprise for us. We went knowing what was in store. We saw Mr. Zimmerman the man we had prayed for in July. He said, "I want you to know the Lord healed me after you anointed me with oil. We are going to Youngstown to the Catherine and Coleman service." Saturday, November 13, Cam Salvaggi and I went to the Presbyterian Hospital to visit Roberta Owen. Cam said to her, "I brought you a gift. The Pastor will tell you about a greater gift." I told her about the love of God. Roberta, her mother Viola and Linda her sister, received Christ as their Savior. Viola said, "If my husband were here, he would receive Christ also."

Tuesday, November 16, we went back to the Pittsburgh Presbyterian Hospital and the father was there. Before we left, he received the Lord Jesus Christ as his Savior. I might say that the Lord called Roberta home to glory, and Robert had become one of my best deacons in the church. Now, Robert has Lou Gehrig disease.

On Friday, October 29, I drove down to the shop. Then I drove to Beaver Falls to visit Brenda and the family. Brent was ill, Brent is my grandson. I had the most wonderful day with them. I said we are going to pray for Brent before we left. Larissa, his sister and my granddaughter, got down on her knees and prayed for her brother. I arrived in Washington two hours later and then Brenda called to tell me that the fever was gone. I believe with all my heart that Larissa's prayer was answered for her brother. God had answered this young lady's prayer.

In 1971, a lady wrecked her car on the street while Dot was taking supplies to the shop in the evening. I tried to help her. I got a double hernia from lifting her up. I said to Dot on the way to church, "I'm really hurt." Monday, Dr. Pizzi said after he examined me, "You have a double hernia." I was admitted into the hospital on Tuesday. Operated on Thursday, Sam Mazzie came up after the Wednesday morning prayer service and said to me, "Jean Harris had a message and interpretation that God healed you." Dr. Pizzi came in with his nurse and examined me and said, "I can not find your hernia on your lower right side. But, we found a small one on the left side." I had surgery and I must say in all honesty and sincerity that the one on the right side was so severe that it pushed through the inner wall. I pushed it back in just before Dr. Bakewell came waling in. The pain was torture, but he couldn't find that one because I know why, God had already revealed it to the prayer group that God had healed me. There was another reason for me to be there. That night after surgery, across my room, I could hear someone crying. I went out to see. I saw a very large lady out there. "May I help you?" I said, she said, "You need help yourself." I insisted and I went in and prayed with the man. A man that was in a coma. I led him to the Lord by having him grip my hands and blink his eyes. He was telling me that he was praying with me. I said, "If Jesus Christ comes into your heart and into your life after we've prayed will you grip my hand?" He griped my hand so hard I thought he was going to dislocate my fingers. They both received Jesus Christ as their Lord and Savior. Two hours later he was dead. That is why the Lord healed one hernia and not both. Jean Harris was right, God did heal me.

Tuesday, May 2, 1971, in the evening Joe Angelilo and I went to visit his daughter-in-law, Donna Angelilo. I had a call from her that her daughter was very ill. When we arrived there at 7:00 p.m., I sat across the room from her and I could hear her heart pound like a locomotive going up a hill. I can honestly say, we anointed her with oil and the pounding stopped. She took her daughter to Dr. Berman and he examined her and gave her a clean bill of health. This child of 6 years of age had open heart surgery when she was 3 years of age. But, what I didn't know until years later when I met the mother Donna, she said the Lord had really healed her heart plus she had allergies and the Lord had healed them also. Glory to his mighty name. Isn't God wonderful. Praise His Holy name.

In the revival of 1971, it was Steve Mark and Tommy Orene and others. We had 175 people saved and all were filled with the Holy Spirit. All across Washington County, as far away as Beaver Falls, West Virginia. We had people that were coming to the services and they were receiving something from God in every service.

Friday, April 12, 1974, Theresa Julian called, her mother was very ill. I drove to the farm to pray. Sister Arena, Theresa was there. After 25 years, I was able to run again. Praise the Lord. I didn't realize it, while I was praying for grandma Arena, Theresa was healed and God healed me without anybody touching me but him. I drove to the Washington hospital to visit someone who was very ill and while I was visiting, it started to rain. When I came outside, my car was just across the lot from the hospital about 70 yards away. I thought, if I could run the way I use to I would go to that automobile and wouldn't even get wet because I was the fastest runner in 5 schools. That still small voice spoke to me and aid, "Why don't you run/" I responded and said, "I can't run." Again, that still small voice said, "Why don't you try." To my amazement, I ran to that automobile and unlocked the door and I sat there and wept before the Lord because God had healed me and I knew it. Praise his Holy name.

In December 1974, Anthony Comfort fell and broke his pelvis. Anthony Comfort was 88 years of age. We visited him and prayed with him and anointed him with oil and the Lord healed him. Two days later he went home from the hospital.

In 1976, we showed a film on the Burning Hell. I invited Marie Hi Smith, a lady who was in and out of the hospital quite frequently. She came to the service and we showed the film "The Burning Hell." Twenty-two people got saved. Marie Hi Smith was number 21. After the service, she went home and a neighbor said to her, "Marie, I hear you went to church." She said, "Yes, I went to church to keep DePolo off my back. He always invited me to church. So, out of the goodness of my heart I went to church." She said, "I hear you went to the altar." She said, "Yes, they had a film." She said, "What was the title of it?" She said, "The Burning Hell." She said, "I hear you went to the altar."

She said, "Yes, I did, that film scared the hell out of me and I went to the altar to give my heart to Jesus." Just a few months later Maria was in the hospital dying. I went in and took a hold of her hand and I said "Maria, aren't you glad that Jesus Christ scared the hell out of you in that film and now you no longer have to fear?" She looked at me and smiled and shortly after Maria Hi Smith went to be with Jesus.

Monday, July 5, I asked June Salvaggi to start the prayer chain over the phone which has been a great asset to our church and to the many whom we pray for. The many who have been healed by the power of God.

Saturday, August 27, 1978, Evelyn Jones called and said her husband had a heart attack. I went to the house and anointed him with oil and prayed with him. He yelled at her for calling me because he said he'd be alright. He broke out in a sweat, and it was hard for him to breathe. After we anointed him it seemed that the perspiration that was so severe stopped. The breathing was normal again. That was on Saturday, on Sunday morning, Albert Jones and his wife came to Sunday school class and to the service. They came to the picnic, because we had a picnic that day at the Washington Park. On Monday, Albert went to the doctor. Dr. Berman, who was the cardiac specialist in Washington. He said to Albert, "You had a heart attack." Albert said, "I know." After examining him and running an EKG on Albert he said, "I can see scar tissue." Albert said, "That tells you one thing doesn't it doctor. God healed me." The doctor said, "I'm going to have to admit you in the hospital." He said, "Oh no, I don't have time. I have to go up and trim Pastor De Polo's shrubbery." The doctor thought that Albert was crazy. When Albert passed away years later he did not die from the heart attack. Later Albert moved to Arizona and Albert had to have a leg amputated because he had a severe case of diabetes. That is what took his life.

On Friday, September 2, 1978, I spoke in the first service at our convention in Philadelphia, Pennsylvania, which was an honor. Anytime your chosen to be a speaker at a convention it is an honor.

In 1978, a young lady by the name of Deborah Carnisky, her maiden name was Deborah Reed, was admitted to the Washington hospital. The doctor said she had temper lob seizure which consisted of inability to handle emotions such as sadness, happiness, excitement, etc. A loss of memory, just a young lady in her early 20's caused by bad adverse reaction to medication. She said, "I also experience motionless state, numbness in the right side of my body, and epileptic seizures." If you weren't careful standing around her, her feet would come up and bop you in the face. "I had severe depression. I thought of killing myself. Loss of speech. One evening I almost died by slipping into and right back out of a coma type state. The doctor told me I was mentally ill. I would be a vegetable and have to be institutionalized. Praise God, I was anointed by Pastor DePolo. God not only saved me but I've been healed. I'm so glad that Jesus Christ is my savior." Praise the Lord. There is nothing our God can't do. There is nothing that he won't do because God loves you and he loves me. He loves us with an everlasting love.

Friday, September 24, 1976, Deloris Gump was healed. It was a Sunday morning in 1978, my sister Mary came with her husband and mother-in-law. She heard the message, she ran to the altar and received Jesus Christ as her Lord and Savior. I prayed for years for Mary to get saved.

Teddy Chechinski was saved Sunday, April 1, 1979, his mother, father, brother, sisters were saved Wednesday, July 29. We saw a miracle. This young man was involved in armed robbery. When he came to the church on a Sunday morning he heard the word of the Lord and he came back that night and God saved him. My wife took a liking to him. He still had to pay for his crime. The judge wanted to send Teddy to prison for 10 years for armed robbery. We attended the trial in Greensburg, Pennsylvania. We were there for 6 hours and we prayed and we prayed and the Judge put me on the stand and I said that he should give this young man another chance because he had received Jesus Christ as his Lord and his Savior and I am sure that God had changed his life. He changes lives completely. The Judge said to me and to others that it had no bearing. Then after the recess, we came back to the trial the Judge said, "You caught me at a weak moment." But, he said that Teddy would spend one year in Camp Hill and he would give Teddy 10 years of probation. The district attorney said, "Don't believe you caught him at a weak moment. He doesn't have a weak moment. Since I've known him, and I'm a Christian, and I know your God delivered him from the Judge's hands." Reminds me of the three Hebrew children in the fiery furnace. My wife Doris would go to the prison Camp Hill in Greensburg, Pennsylvania. She would bring her implements with her and go behind the bars and cut Teddy's hair. The warden would say to her, "Aren't you really related to him?" She would say, "No, we are not related. I'm the Pastors wife." He said to her, "I've been here for 30 years and I've never seen love like this manifested in anyone. Not even in the family that comes to visit." Today Teddy is married, a graduate of Elan Bible College. They have 4 children and the Lord has blessed him in a mighty way.

Another beautiful thing happened in 1975, Tina Clutter was a young lady in the Washington Hospital depressed area, in the 3A's mental ward. I would visit Tina everyday, but she was getting no better. I'm sure because of drugs her mind was about gone. One day she said to me, "You know something Pastor, I'm Jesus Christ." The next day she was someone else. I just about gave up on her but the spirit moved upon me to visit her this day. We prayed again and again and The lord delivered her in a marvelous way. Because of her love of Christ, she was able to win her mother, her grandmother, her grandfather, aunts, uncles, all in all. The last account I had, she was responsible for 125 souls coming to Jesus Christ. Our church was in the spirit of revival.

Friday, September 7, we had a seven hour prayer meeting in church.

Tuesday, September 25, 1979 at 4:00, CB a woman I love dearly in the Lord called to tell me her husband had suffered a severe heart attack and was not expected to live the night. I went to the hospital immediately. They were bringing her husband back into the coronary Intensive Care room. CB said to me, "He's not saved. Go in and get him to accept Jesus as his Savior." I went in but the nurse was working on him. I was not able to speak to him or pray with him. Then it happened. I saw the monitor go blank, and then she came into the room. The nurse saw what had happened and called for help. CB said to me, "Pray, pray, God will bring him back long enough to receive Christ." We prayed and to my amazement, I saw the doctor and other doctors come in and they asked us to leave the room. I waited near the door. I heard Doctor Badiali say, "It's amazing." He started to breathe again and they did not have to shock him back. God did all this. Doctor Badiali came in and said, "This evening your husband was dead. It is amazing, his heart is in perfect rhythm, but I don't expect him to live the night." I spoke up and said, "Don't believe this." I went in and said to Guss, the husband, "Did you hear us pray?" He said, "No." How could he, he was dead. Their son Bob, the daughter June, and the grandson Robert who was also a doctor was there. Guss excepted Christ as his Savior. He lived for 2 1/2 years. When the Lord took him, he was calling upon the name of Jesus Christ and speaking in other tongues and speaking solely to God and God took him home to Glory. Praise God forever. Because our Friday night prayer and fasting lasted 7 years. Our convention was in Pittsburgh, a young man by the name of George Chicora, a business man, and his beautiful wife, Darlene, a school teacher, were on the verge of divorce. We prayed with them at the convention and today they are very happy in the Lord. The Lord is using them to witness to the people that they sell monuments because they bought the Kurtz Monument Company. They witnessed to each home that they went into and they have won many people to the Lord. They have a beautiful daughter Beth, who has a beautiful voice and she's entered college. She has a voice like an Angel. Thank God for his everlasting burst in love that he's bestowed upon us. Praise the name of the Lord forever.

Ronnie Bloom, who was a very dear friend of mine, owns 5 tire business's. Ronnie had surgery on Monday, January 20, for cancer. His mother would call me and say, "Please Reverend, pray for Ronnie because the Rabbi doesn't know how to get in touch with God." One day she called me in the middle of February and we prayed together and the next thing I knew, Ronnie was healed by the power of God. We experienced a rival in our midst in the month of April. Seventy people were saved in the year 1980. We had 171 conversions and 88 Baptism's. In 1988, the Lord gave me a message for Ronnie, the man who was healed of cancer. I went to Ronnie and I said to him, "Ronnie, the Lord had given me a message for you." He said, "What is the message Pastor?" I said, "It's not a good one. It's a hard one. God has said I have healed you of cancer, but you did not heed my warning. I spoke to you again and again, but your turned a deaf ear to me. Now all that you've gained and prospered you will lose. Turn to me, turn to me even in this hour and I will repent of the things that will come your way." So, Ronnie has not turned to God. Ronnie has not looked at him and now Ronnie is down to 1 business.

December 1980, we went to the Holy Land. On Friday, December 5, on the Mount of Olives, I started to praise the Lord and suddenly I felt a great power move over my inner most being. I never felt anything like this in all my Christian life. That was in 1980.

Friday, May 7, an all night prayer service. Sunday, May 9, seventeen saved and two baptisms. Ella was healed of a hernia June 24. June 24, Gladys was healed of a hernia. Sunday, June 27, one hundred and one were saved in 1982. Seventy one were filled with the Spirit. Tuesday, July 14, on vacation in Virginia Beach, after we left the beach, Doris wanted to go to the Linhaven Mall, which is outside Virginia Beach. She went shopping about 5:00 p.m. after we ate dinner. I went outside to sit on the bench watching the buses bring people into the mall. Where I sat on the bench was a black lady. She looked at me and I observed her. I noticed she had a walker. She said, "I'm waiting for a minister from Pennsylvania. The Lord spoke to me this morning and told me where to sit, this minister from Pennsylvania is going to come over and pray for me." I said, "I'm the minister from Pennsylvania." She said, "Will you please pray for me. God told me this morning when I tossed and turned that you would pray for me and that he would heal me." I looked at her and raised my right hand above her head and I laid my hand on her head and I could feel the power of God going through my hands. She fell back. I didn't know what people would think. Then she started to cry. I didn't know what to say or what to do. A few minutes later, a car drove up. They were going to help this lady get into the car. To my amazement she cried out in a loud voice. "The Lord has healed me. Didn't I tell you that God was going to heal me." For 6 years she was unable to walk. She had been injured in a car accident. She walked without help to the car. All the people in the car started to praise God. What a feeling. I didn't even tell my wife this because I was afraid that she would think I had lost my mind or something had happened to me. Praise God for his mercy and his goodness.

In 1982, one hundred and five were baptized through the Holy Spirit and forty three were saved. I made 5,289 visits to homes, hospitals, jails and institutions. My prayers will always be that God will use me as his instrument when I visit the sick to raise them up for the Glory of God. Not for my Glory, but for his Glory.

Monday, April 16, 1990, Gracy Megyesy, a young lady from our church, was healed from inner blood clots. God had healed her. She went back to the doctor and the doctor confirmed this. She came back to the church a week later and we prayed for her again. It was on a Sunday night, standing in front of the altar in front of the communion table. Gracy had a hearing problem from an automobile accident. It was getting worse. The doctors said they would have to operate. She came up to the altar and we prayed for her. God laid his hand on her, the hearing aide popped out. When the hearing aide popped out, Gracy fell to the floor. When she fell to the floor, after awhile we helped her up. She said, "You don't know what happened do you?" I said, "I believe I do. I saw the hearing aide pop out." She said,

"That's right. I can hear you whisper. God has healed my hearing. He's healed my ears." Praise the name of the Lord. I can remember, it was on a Sunday morning in 1982, because God gave me this gift in 1980 and I know nothing about it until later on in February 1981, I was ministering to people in the Sanctuary upstairs. The church was packed. At 1:00 in the afternoon, we had about 40-50 people lying on the floor and they covered each and every one of them. Janet Rizak, the Sunday school teacher, was downstairs teaching the children in the junior church. She realized it was 1:00 and there had to be something drastically wrong. She sent upstairs a child and she said, "You go up there and see what Brother DePolo is doing. See why he is keeping the people so late." The child came up and peaked through the glass door and ran back downstairs and said, "Teacher, teacher." She said, "What's wrong?" He said, "I don't know what is going on. Brother DePolo is up there killing them all. They are all covered over with covers."

When I was injured in the mines, just a teenager, my left leg was 2 inches shorter than my right. It got so bad that I thought my hip was going to break. So, August 2, 1990, I went to the hospital in Beaver County, where my son-in-law is also on the staff, Brenda's husband,

Dr. Kludo, and he introduced me to Dr. Michael Zernich, who is an orthopedic surgeon. Dr. Zernich was getting ready to operate on me. I looked up and I said to him, "How long will it be?" He said, "Just a few minutes." I looked up again. I couldn't see Dr. Zernich, I could see someone all dressed in white hovering over me. Later on, the surgery went so beautifully that Dr. Zernich couldn't understand what had happened. He said to me later, and I told him about the vision that I had, I couldn't see him. I saw a person all dressed in white. Dr. Zernich looked at me and he said, "You know, I wish I would of known that last night because I would have slept. I had a sleepless night. Your hip was one of the worst mangled hips I've ever had to work on. Every part that we put into that hip fit perfect like it was made for you." After surgery, July 21, 1990, I've never had an ache or pain with that hip. Where my leg was 2-2 1/2 inches shorter than my right, my left leg, now my legs are even. Most recently, 2 1/2 months ago, I had surgery on my right knee. I guess because the way I had to walk and arthritis set in. They had to move the knee cap. I had to have that done. After surgery they brought me back to my room and I couldn't move my legs. I didn't realize, that's because I had the type of surgery that I did. Two nights later, I asked the nurse to turn out the lights. They kept wanting me to take medication for pain and the only pain I had was with my ligaments. The same way with my hip, never any pain from the surgery. I asked the nurse to turn out the lights and she did. I had a group of people who came to visit me from our church in Washington. While they are visiting with me, they had balloons sent in. "Get well soon", "hurry up and recover", and etc. After they left, about 11:00 at night, I looked up at the balloon and lo and behold, it was the face of the evil one. I looked up again and there he was. I said, "Oh, your up there. Don't you realize that greater is he that is in me than he that is in the world." I looked again and it was gone. I had chills. I thought maybe I was becoming feverish. I asked the nurse to come in. She did, to see if I had and said, "No." She checked my temperature and she said, "No, you're not fevered." I asked her to turn out the light. Outside of my room, as I was looking out over the lawn, there was a man all dressed in white with his hands raised. Now I know why Lucifer didn't stick around. I know, because my Lord had delivered me out of his hands many times. Praise the name of the Lord. Praise the name of the Lord forever. I thank God that the second operation has been a tremendous success too. I know that the hand of the Lord is upon me, just like he promised it would always be. All he wants us to do is to love him and serve him and live for him all the days of our lives. Since 1964, I've kept a diary. My visits from 1964-1987 to hospitals, jails, homes 123,191 thousand, Holy Spirit baptisms in those 7 years 729, salvation 11,000, all together from 1964-1990, 139,392 thousand visits, 775 funerals, 350 weddings, God has really been good to us. God has really blessed our ministry in a special mighty and unique way.

In the year that I was saved, 1953, as I said, my daughter Brenda and her persistency not wanting to go to church without me led me to the Lord. It brought me to the knowledge of Jesus Christ. Two weeks before that, we were still living in Meadowbrook, West Virginia, there was a gentleman that always caused me problems and troubles and trials and tribulations. I thought the best way to remedy this, we both worked at the mines, we both operated those motors or locomotives they called them, I thought when he passed by, I had a 38 and he always slowed down there while I was hiding behind a tree, that I was going to finish it once and for all and they would never know who it was. I was waiting, waiting, waiting. I quit work at 11:00. At 12:00 I was home and I was waiting because I knew he quit an hour after I did. I waited and waited and he never came. I never

113

realized why. God had a hand in it because their motor wrecked and they worked all night trying to put it on. About 12:30 a fear come over me. I could hear my mother singing, "I'm praying for you, I'm praying for you." The gun I held in my hand fell to the ground. I picked it up and I threw it in the Sulfur Creek. I thank God that I had a praying mother. I thank God that I had a daughter who was very persistent. I can see in my daughter and I can see in my son the Glory of God. I pray as you read this that it will encourage you to seek his face and to go all the way with the Lord Jesus Christ in the manner that I had. I had never been sorry because God has blessed my wife and I with 2 beautiful children, 5 grandchildren, and four great-grandchildren. Praise the name of the Lord forever.

I've had one of the greatest Deacon boards that you could ever expect to have. A spiritual board and a Deaconess board. Beautiful ladies that really know how to pray and get a hold of God. I thank God for the manner that he has blessed our work and our church. I thank God for Jesus Christ who suffered, bled and died that we might have life, and life more abundantly. Yes, I don't want to rust out. No, no, I want to continue to do my best for him because he gave his best for me. Praise the name of the Lord.

Our son Frank is pastoring a church in Belle Vernon, Pennsylvania which is about 20-22 miles from us. Our daughter Brenda, I had the privilege of marrying Brenda a few years ago to Dr. Kludo in Beaver Falls. Brenda has a son who is an emergency room physician. She has a daughter that is a dedicated school teacher also with a Masters Degree. So, God has blessed our daughter and our son. Our son has two sons, the oldest grandson, Phillip, whom I gave his first football, he has a son Jonathan, he has a daughter at home, Heather. Jonathan is a body builder in California, he is doing quite well, Phillip has a good job here in Pennsylvania. Above all, our daughter Brenda married Dr. Ron Kludo from Beaver Falls. Most recently, Dr. Kludo received Christ as his Lord and Savior. He reminds me of yours truly. When he's alone all he wants to do is read his Bible. When he's with people all he wants is people that are knowledgeable about the Bible to ask questions about the Bible. I know that this is a young man that God is going to use. So, I want you to remember Dr. Kludo when you pray, that God will use him for his honor and for his glory. I can see my daughter drawing closer and closer to the Lord. It's all because we learn to lean closer and closer to the Lord. My wife and I will continue in the ministry of the Lord, because Doris loves the Lord with all of her heart too, we will continue the ministry that God has given us until God calls us home. Praise the name of the Lord forever!

I thank God that my son Frank felt the calling of the Lord at a young age and went to Bible Seminary to become a Minister in 1959. He has three lovely children, Philip Donald, Jonathan Frank and Heather Rae. He and his wife Rebecca live and pastor the covenant Christian Church in Belle Vernon. Pastor Frank also travels abroad teaching the word of God. He also has a Doctorate in Theology.

In 1993, I met a wonderful person by the name of Rita Skittle. She was the daughter of Caesar Falcone of Canonsburg, PA. Rita was a great business woman, unfortunately, she suffered a severe stroke and was paralyzed. I recommended a young lady from our church to work for her and assist her in her home, her name was Carolyn Sprowls became a born again Christian and really loved the Lord with all of her heart. In 1995, my wife and I were in Florida, visiting our daughter and son-in-law we received a phone call that Rita had passed away. She touched all of our lives dearly and we miss her very much.

TESTIMONY OF CAROLYN SPROWLS

In October 1963, I found out I had a tumor on my right ovary which weighed approximately 5 1/2 pounds. I was sixteen years old and the tumor was malignant.

I was put into Washington hospital, but not told I had cancer (only that they were going to operate and remove a tumor).

My mother was not save (nor I) and she was going around frantically seeking prayer from people. A short time before my grandfather (my mothers dad) was in the hospital in the same room with Rev. Joe Marasco who told my mother about Rev. John DePolo's church and my mother contacted them and the church immediately started praying for me (someone they didn't even know).

My mother Dorothy Yaquinto was praying and begging God to heal me (She was not saved). Praying one day in front of her kitchen stove she was asking God to heal me and an electric shock went through her. She finally said, "God even you don't heal my daughter, I will serve you." Instantly she was saved. God spoke to her and she went around telling everyone, "I was healed." Everyone thought my mother was crazy.

The doctors removed the tumor out of me and when testing the blood they could find no cancer. It was a while before my mother finally told me. She was afraid to tell me I had cancer, but she made me go to church. I was very rebellious, but as I kept going the spirit got a hold of me and I came into the realness of Jesus Christ.

I thank God for Rev. DePolo. How he goes and prays for people he doesn't even know. He did a favor for my grandmother and she was saved also just because of that favor.

The example he has taught me (his love for Jesus) has been impressed deep within my heart and life.

He has made me realize and care where souls spend eternity and as he always says, "Only one life will soon be past only whats done for Christ will last. What are we going to take with us?"

I often wonder if Rev. DePolo didn't go and pray for people like he does, "Would I be saved today?"

If ever there was an example in my life a legacy (of teaching me to love the savior with every thing that is in me) a hero. Reverend DePolo is mine.

I spoke about this to many of my friends, and they thought that I should put this in my book. (I remember that night in November, that

I was going to commit murder. I had this plan in my mind for many weeks, and I waited for the opportune time, the person that I was angry with was one of my best friends, or that is what I thought.

I loved to gamble in those days, and he was always with me, and every move I made he was there, and he was the fellow that kept my wife posted about my different affairs and many things he adds without validity.

So this Friday night I thought it would be the perfect time for me to kill him. I came home from work at 11:30 p.m. and after 12:30 a.m., Doris and the children were in bed, and I went on my way to wait for him because I knew the hour that he would be passing by. I waited and my thoughts were that once and for all, I would get rid of my so called friend.

He was always telling my father about my gambling, and my father was a constant nag toward me, he was always taking sides with my wife. I thought about this, and I thought about our two wonderful children that God had given us, but Satan had blinded me. I waited and waited for my so called friend to come by. I waited and it seemed like weeks. The longer I waited the angrier I became. I was going to empty that 38 in his body and then throw away the gun in the river, so I thought.

It was now 2:30 a.m. He still hadn't come by, and I was starting to get cold, but I was dressed warm and I was drinking my wine as usual as I waited. Then a strange thing happened. We have a song in our hymnal and realized that after this I started to church, I could hear my mother saying to me, "Son, I am praying for you."

Chills ran up and down my spine, my hands started to tremble, my body was shaking like someone caught in a windstorm. I started to cry, and I couldn't understand what was happening. What I didn't know, the Bible says that God will watch over them that are heirs of salvation. I looked at the gun in my hand and fear came into me in such a manner as I have never known. I threw the gun in to the river, and I couldn't wait to go home. The next morning I went over to visit with mom and dad. My mother took me aside so father wouldn't hear, and she said, "God laid you upon my heart last night. I prayed for you until 2:30 a.m. Then God blessed my soul and I was able to sleep. Please tell me what have you been up to." I lied to my mother. I said, "Everything is fine.

Reverend Corsini came to our home many times after that to get us to attend church. We started going to church, but it didn't last too long because I looked at people instead of looking at Jesus Christ. That is what my mother said to me, "Don't look at people, look at the Lord. He will help you my son. God loves you and your family.

The gentleman that I tried to kill became my best friend indeed after all I had been through with him down through the years. Now we are good friends. We went to the place where they were playing poker and we got into the game.

After playing for about 3 hours, a fight started and my friend and I got under the table. The man of the house got his 30-30 rifle and he was going to start shooting, but another man by the name of Mack Rachel pulled out his 45 and made all of us get on our

knees. He was after the man with the rifle. He knew that he was going to shoot him. So my friend Frank hit him with his chair and he kept Mr. Mack from committing murder. After the game, I went home. Doris was very angry at me and wanted to take the children and leave. My mother came to our house and once again she started her 30 second sermon with me, "Son, I am praying for you." God had me on my knees again last night. When will you wake up. Can't you see the enemy of your soul is trying to destroy you and your family. One day Doris will leave you with the children and then what will you do?"

I drove Mr. Seals home and I thanked the Lord that he didn't die while I was with him, because I was afraid of death or anyone dying in my presence. My sister-in-law was working in their home and she told us after he passed away that he was begging the Lord Christ to have mercy on him. He screamed and wailed, but the Lord didn't answer. Finally, Mr. Seals screamed, "The devil is here with chains, will somebody please help me because God won't answer. I know I have committed the unpardonable sin." She said he died screaming, "The devil is coming after me."

For days after the funeral I couldn't sleep, but didn't tell anyone. Again my mother came into our home and said to me, "When will you start to listen? God spoke to me again about you. Son, I am praying for you." I wanted to scream, "Please leave me alone", but at that time, our son Frankie came into the house. What I didn't know why I was fighting conviction in the worst way. I was very stubborn and I wouldn't yield.

I was about 14 years of age, my father made a 30 gallon barrel of wine from blackberries for my sister Ann's wedding, which was in the fall. I would go down to the cellar and put the hose in the barrel and cipher wine from the barrel. I did this for many months not realizing that one day the barrel would be empty.

After about 6 months or less, one day before the wedding as they were making plans, father and John, Ann's husband to be, said to me, "Let's go down and open the wine barrel so that we can have all things ready for the wedding."

I started to leave but father said to me, "Where are you going. We need your help in the cellar." They went down and carried the empty barrel out of the cellar and I must say I never saw my father as angry as he was now. I really liked the taste of wine. My mother came to my rescue and said probably my buddies drank the wine. But, God knows that I drank every gallon.

The reason I am telling you this is so that you will know that God can break any fetter and chain and set you free, (John 6:63 - It is the spirit that gives life - He is the life giver. And ye shall know the truth and the truth shall set you free). (John 8:36). I learned this truth from my mother.

At the age of 17, I started working in the mines thinking that I knew it all. One day a good friend and I went to the movies in Clarksburg. After the movies, we went to a beer-garden and we drank beer until midnight. We caught the street car for home because we were too drunk to walk home. We started to walk in the snow and we were too drunk. We passed out on the main highway. At that time, there were very few cars and we were alive because of God. I know he spared my life many times. After about 15-20 minutes, Pat Marra comes along and he pulled Buster Young and me off the highway. I said to Pat: "Please don't take me home, my father will kill me. Take me to my sisters, Evelyn Secreto's house." They thought I was dead because my body was as stiff as a board. The alcohol that we had in our body kept us from freezing to death. I promised my sister and brother-in-law Pat, that I would never get drunk again. Until the next time, which was a few days away. (Thank God for Jesus Christ who can break any fetter).

"A teacher who had her collarbone broken in an auto accident was prayed for and the doctor took her arm out of the sling the next day. A student who was seeking the Lord for a fuller Christian life was filled with the Holy Spirit in a classroom at the local high school. One drug addict was saved and filled with the Holy Spirit the same night. He returned to the services the next week with his father. The sharing never stops because the Holy Spirit will not allow it. And so it goes on and on.

"I personally have benefited from these services because, through them, I have been led to learn of the ministry that God would have through me. It has been fantastically exciting; and the best thing is that God's prophecies are that this will expand to reach our community. With God all things are possible!!

"Throughout all this excitement the biggest lesson to learn is that we who receive from God's Treasure House share a responsibility to use the gifts He has given... to share them with those who are open...and, most important, to learn more about them.

"My prayer is that God, in his infinite wisdom, will lead all of us to dig into His work more vigorously, to pray more fervently, and to listen to His still small voice more carefully than ever before."

Rev. John DePolo, pastor, comments about the move of God:

"What is Revival? It is not merely an evangelistic or healing campaign. Neither is it a moving of the Spirit upon the ungodly. Reviving comes through the Holy Spirit; He is the great Reviver.

How miraculously He can refresh us and put new strength in our lives when it seems we have reached a state of spiritual collapse, He is the Spirit of quickening.

"Even though there is much apostasy in these days, we can look for gracious blessings from heaven. God has spoken through His prophet Joel, 'I will pour out of my Spirit upon all flesh; and your sons and your daughters shall prophesy, your old men shall dream dreams, your young men shall see visions; and also upon the servants and upon the handmaids in those days will I pour out of my Spirit. And I will show wonders...before the great and terrible day of the Lord come' (Joel 2:28-31).

"This outpouring will be upon "all flesh." A mightier moving of the Spirit than the world has ever known. This is happening in the Christian Church of North America in Washington, Pennsylvania. Every Sunday night the Lord fills young people that are seeking, knocking, and asking. From September through December 1970 we have seen 54 young people receive the Baptism in the Holy Spirit. Many have been saved and others healed by the power of God.

GOD IS MOVING BY HIS SPIRIT

REVIVAL BEING EXPERIENCED IN WASHINGTON, PENNSYLVANIA CHURCH

The Christian Church of North America in Washington, Pennsylvania has been experiencing a mighty outpouring of the Holy Spirit for the past several months. The report below is a compilation of some of the material which has reached the editor's desk. You will note that there has been very little editorial adjustment. We wanted you to read the stories just as they reached us. I am grateful to Rev. John DePolo, pastor of the church, and Pat Farrell and Samuel Mazzie who supplied most of the information.

Here is what Pat Farrell had to say about the move of God's Spirit in the church:

"This story has been a long time in coming, but it seems that every time a chapter is finished, we find that it is only beginning. In fact, no one even seems to know where or when the whole thing began. One thing is sure, a Revival has started in the Christian Church of North

America in Washington, Pennsylvania and it just will not stop! Hallelujah!

"If a beginning had to be given this story, I suppose it would lay in the hopes and prayers of some faithful prayer warriors who, nearly two years ago asked God to pour out His Holy Spirit on the children of our church and community. Despite a seemingly endless streak of no results, these people clung to a repeated prophecy that God would shower our young people with His Holy Spirit.

"Since the fall of 1970 when the first fruits began to appear, literally hundreds of people, adults and teens alike have entered the church to leave with new life. It would take hours to cite every miracle, every healing and in filling of the Holy Spirit, therefore only a few cases will be mentioned. Behind these lay many more just as real - just as exciting.

"Drugs seem to be one of the biggest problems inherent in the youth of our community, and so the total reformation of a three-year drug user was one fantastic place for the Holy Spirit to begin His blessings. When this boy found Jesus Christ as his own Saviour and received all that Jesus had for him, including the baptism in the Holy Spirit, all Heaven seemed to break loose. Interspersed with "born again" addicts, the youth of the church who had always been "typical church kids", began to find the same news power in their lives. Together these teens have literally gone into their high schools and brought their friends to the Sunday night services. And the most amazing things have happened: these strangers to the church have also been blessed with salvation and the infilling of the Holy Spirit. When God said that every man was accounted as being equal, He wasn't kidding.

"In the month of January and February 1971, we have seen thirty-seven receive the Baptism in the Holy Spirit, and many have been saved, a young man was saved, baptized in the Holy Spirit, and healed of asthma in a moment of time.

:Revival is like a consuming fire. Once it begins to burn, spiritual fire spreads rapidly, increasing in intensity with the addition of further fuel and the quickening of gracious providential winds.

"The conviction of sinners is not revival, but rather the product of revival. When sinners observe the earnestness of believers, they repent and turn to God. It may be noted that the salvation of souls is almost invariably the result of revival. This sequence is indicated in the dispensations setting of spiritual awakening described by the prophet Joel and quoted by Peter on the day of Pentecost:

"I will pour out my Spirit…and it shall come to pass, that whosoever shall call on the name of the Lord shall be saved. For the promise is unto you, and your children, and to all that are afar off, even as many as the Lord our God shall call.

(Acts 2:39)."

Just as we were preparing this article for type setting the following report was received by the editor:

On Sunday night March 7, 1971, the Christian Church of North America, Washington, Pennsylvania were hosts to the Campus Life singers and musicians. This group is made up of high school students who have dedicated their talents to winning other students to Jesus Christ.

The Campus Life singers are directed by a high school teacher with a major in music and youth for Christ directors who planned the service. After the main program, an invitation was given to those who wanted to receive Jesus Christ. Many responded and were led to the

Lord by the singing group of which several have received the Holy Spirit Baptism.

After the audience was dismissed, a good number stayed on for blessings from God. Several received the baptism in the Holy Spirit. Since September 20, 1970 we have had over 105 baptisms in the Holy Spirit. These are mainly youth and are from all denominations.

The Spirit of the Lord continues here and there seems to be no let-up. We praise God for confirming his works with signs following the ministry. We are looking for greater blessings from God. Note: As of March 21, 1971, 110 have been filled with the Holy Spirit.

A few weeks after that I was injured in the mines. My hip was fractured. I didn't know it then, but I found out to my dismay that my leg would be 2 1/2 inches shorter than my right leg. Oh, that pain; day and night. There was no let up in the pain. I lost 40 pounds after about 30 days. The doctor would give me medicine, but the pain was so severe that I could not sleep night or day for 30 days. One day my mother started to read

me the Gospel of St. John and immediately the pain left. After she would stop reading, the pain would return. I would say to my mother: "Read to me the Gospel of St. John". I can surely say the pain would leave. But, then mother would say, "It is time for your father to come home from work". You see, my father was a devout Catholic and they were not permitted to read the Bible. The doctor said to me, "You will never walk again". My godly mother would say in front of him, "Don't believe him. God is going to heal you". So, I promised the Lord that I would serve him and start going to church. After a few weeks I was able to walk, I said to my Mother, "I am too young to go to church". She was very disappointed, but she said she would keep on praying for me, which she did every day.

After limping and wearing a built up shoe of 2 1/2 inches for 50 years, our daughters husband Dr. Ron Kludo, a doctor in Beaver Falls, said to me, "Dr. Zernich is a great doctor. He can make you well again from the terrible limp." So, in August 1990, Dr. Zernich operated on me, and I had no aches or pain from the surgery. Just as he was about to put me under, I asked him how long it would be. He said, "A few minutes". I looked up again, but I couldn't see the doctor. I saw a person standing tall and dressed in white.

I told Dr. Zernich and he said, "I wish I had known that last night, then I wouldn't of worried so much. I could of had a good nights sleep. (Jesus was there). No aches or no pain after surgery.

April 23, 1992, I had a knee replacement. Again, I had no pain after surgery. The enemy appeared the 3rd night, but in a few minutes he left. Then I realized why he left so suddenly. The Lord Jesus Christ was standing outside my window with his hands toward me. I thank God for Jesus Christ who could take a sinner like me and make a candidate of heaven out of him. Praise the Lord anyhow.

In 1998, my daughter located our family in Cerenzia, Italy. Cerenzia is a village in the mountains of Calabria. Brenda, Ron and I finally had the privilege of going there to meet the DePaola family (our first, second and third cousins) of about 60 to 70 wonderful, warm and hospitable family members. I walked on the streets that my father and mother lived on. I went into the house that I was born in and also went to visit the church that my sister, Evelyn, Anna and I were baptized in. What a wonderful feeling to be there with my family. I prayed and read the bible to them. Many of my cousins then accepted the Lord as their savior and welcomed our prayers. We are in touch with them and have been there to visit this past summer once again.

In July, 1999, I retired from being the pastor of the Christian Church of North America in Washington, PA after pastoring for 38

133

1/2 years. I now dedicate all of my time to visiting the hospitals and convalescent homes daily.

I thank the Lord for all that he has done for me and my family.

Back of Book

Rev. De Polo was born in Cerenzia, Calabria Italy on June 3, 1920 to Francesco and Francesca De Polo. His father, Francesco had such a desire to live in America that he brought his family, John being six months old at the time and arrived in America. The family relocated in West Virginia. Rev. De Polo's father became a coal miner in order to support his family of three children at this time. When John was 18 years of age, he also became a coal miner.

In 1953, he became a Christian and gave his heart to the Lord. He had great experiences of being a Christian and wanted to share his love and knowledge of the Lord. He then studied for the Ministry. John pastored for more than 45 years and has many friends from all of these years in West Virginia, Pennsylvania and Washington. He now has a visitation ministry in the nursing homes and hospitals, as God continues to bless him at age 82.

Printed in the United States
759200004B